THE
NIGHT SKY

A Guide to the Stars

By Ian Ridpath
Illustrated by Wil Tirion

Running Press
Philadelphia, Pennsylvania

First published in the United States of America in 1994 by
Running Press Book Publishers.

Text copyright © 1985, 1994 by Ian Ridpath
Illustration copyright © 1985, 1994 by Wil Tirion

Originally published by HarperCollins Publishers Limited under the
title *Collins Gem Night Sky*

9 8 7 6 5 4 3 2 1
Digit on the right indicates the number of this printing.

ISBN: 1-56138-386-4

Library of Congress Cataloging-in-Publication Number: 93-085525

Cover design by Toby Schmidt
Cover photo, *The Pleiades in Taurus*, courtesy of California Institute
of Technology

Printed in Italy by Amadeus S.p.A.

This book may be ordered by mail from your publisher. Please
include $2.50 for postage and handling. *But try your bookstore first!*

Running Press Book Publishers
125 South Twenty-second Street
Philadelphia, Pennsylvania 19103-4399

Contents

How to use this book

This book contains individual charts of the 88 constellations that fill the entire sky (in alphabetical order). All the stars marked on the charts are visible to the naked eye under clear skies, but in towns, where the skies are polluted by dirt and the glare from streetlights, binoculars may be necessary to pick out the faintest stars shown. In addition to the naked-eye stars, the maps mark the location of other important objects such as star clusters, nebulae, and galaxies; most of these require some form of optical aid to be seen. Specific areas of interest in certain constellations (such as the Pleiades, page 213), are shown in greater detail on larger-scale maps, which include fainter stars than on the main charts.

Each constellation is accompanied by descriptions of the main objects of interest to the amateur observer, with an indication of the type of instrument and the magnification needed to see them. The majority of objects described are within the range of small telescopes (i.e. telescopes whose front lens has an aperture of 50–60 mm).

The position of the constellations in relation to each other can be found from a ten-page mini-atlas of the entire sky on pages 28–37.

This book is usable anywhere in the world, although not all constellations will be visible from any given place, e.g. constellations in the south polar region of the sky will always remain below the horizon for mid-northern latitude observers, and vice versa.

Introduction

The sky is divided up into 88 areas, known as *constellations*, which serve as a convenient way of locating the position of objects in the sky. The stars of a constellation usually have no physical connection between one another: although they appear in the same direction in the sky, they are actually at vastly differing distances from us.

Constellations come in many different shapes and sizes. The largest constellation, Hydra, the water snake, is a long and rambling figure that covers an area of sky 19 times greater than that of the smallest constellation. Crux, the Southern Cross. Some constellations consist of easily recognisable patterns of bright stars, such as Orion, while others are faint and difficult to identify.

The tradition of dividing the sky into constellations began thousands of years ago when ancient peoples assigned certain star patterns the names of their gods, heroes, and fabled animals. With few exceptions, the star patterns bear very little resemblance to the people and creatures they are supposed to represent; the connections are symbolic rather than literal.

The ancient Greeks recognized a total of 48 constellations, including the 12 constellations of the *zodiac*, through which the Sun passes on its yearly path around the sky. (The Sun's path, known as the

5

ecliptic, is plotted on the maps in this book as a dashed line.) Various other constellations were added at later times.

Early celestial cartographers drew the constellation figures as they pleased, for there was no standardized shape for each one, nor was there even a generally agreed list of constellations. Each cartographer was free to introduce new constellations of his own invention, and to amend or omit the inventions of

Quadrans Muralis, an old constellation that once occupied a place above the head of Boötes, as shown on the 1801 star atlas of Johann Bode. *Royal Greenwich Observatory.*

others. Constellation figures frequently overlapped one another, and sometimes stars were shared between two constellations.

This state of confusion persisted until 1930 when the International Astronomical Union, astronomy's governing body, adopted the list of 88 constellations that we know today, and set down their exact boundaries. There is no particular reason why we should have 88 constellations, or why they should be the shape they are. Rather like the political map of the world, the subdivision of the sky is an accident of history. But unlike the countries of the world, the names and the borders of the constellation are not likely to change until the slow, steady movements of the stars, known as their *proper motions*, render the existing constellation shapes unrecognizable, thousands of years from now.

Star brightness

Star brightnesses are expressed in terms of *magnitudes* (abbreviated mag.). This system was started by the Greek astronomer Hipparchus in the second century B.C. He divided the stars into six categories of brightness, from the brightest stars (first magnitude), to the faintest stars that he could see (sixth magnitude). Nowadays star brightenesses are measured to thenearest hundredth of a magnitude by sensitive instruments known as photometers. A difference of five magnitudes is now defined as being exactly equal to a brightness difference of 100 times;

consequently, each magnitude step is equal to the 5th root of 100, which is approximately 2.5. The table (page 9) shows the difference in brightness that corresponds to a given magnitude difference. Stars over 2.5 times brighter than mag. 1 are given negative (minus) magnitues, e.g. Sirius, the brightest star in the sky, which has a magnitude of −1.46. Stars fainter than 6th mag. are given progressively larger positive magnitudes. The faintest objects seen through telescopes on Earth have magnitudes of about 24. The constellation charts in this book are complete down to mag. 5.5; the total number of stars shown on them is approximately 3000. The sky atlas section of the book shows stars down to mag. 4.5.

The magnitude of diffuse objects such as star clusters, nebulae, galaxies, and comets is more difficult to quantify than that of a star. A diffuse object's brightness is usually given as though all its light were concentrated into one star-like point.

Therefore a galaxy of 9th-mag. appears of the same brightness as would an out-of-focus star of 9th mag., whose light was spread over the same area as the galaxy. The best way to estimate the brightness of diffuse objects is to compare them with the image of an out-of-focus star of known magnitude.

Conversion of magnitude difference into brightness difference

Difference in magnitude	Difference in brightness
0.5	1.6
1.0	2.5
1.5	4.0
2.0	6.3
2.5	10
3.0	16
3.5	25
4.0	40
5.0	100
6.0	250
7.5	1000
10	10,000
12.5	100,000
15	1,000,000

Star names

There are several different systems for identifying stars, as a result of which a given star may be referred to in more than one way. Many of the brightest stars have proper names, which are of Arabic, Greek, and Latin origin; examples are Altair, Sirius, and Regulus, respectively. Another common system is to give the brightest stars in each constellation a Greek letter; this system was started in 1603 by the German celestial cartographer Johann Bayer, so that the Greek letters attached to stars are known as Bayer letters. For example, Sirius is also known as α (alpha) Canis Majoris, meaning that is is the star α (alpha) in the constellation Canis Major (note that the genitive form of the constellation's name is always used when referring to a star by its Bayer letter). Stars that are not identified in either of these ways may be given a number, called a Flamsteed number (e.g. 19 Lyncis), first introduced in a catalog compiled by the first English Astronomer Royal John Flamsteed (1646–1719). Fainter stars are referred to by their numbers in any one of several star catalogs.

Greek alphabet

α	alpha	ι	iota	ρ	rho
β	beta	κ	kappa	σ	sigma
γ	gamma	λ	lambda	τ	tau
δ	delta	μ	mu	υ	upsilon
ε	epsilon	ν	nu	φ	phi
ζ	zeta	ξ	xi	χ	chi
η	eta	ο	omicron	ψ	psi
θ	theta	π	pi	ω	omega

Various astronomers have also compiled specialized lists of particular types of stars, such as double stars, nearby stars, white dwarf stars, and these provide another source of nomenclature. In this book, some double stars cataloged by the Russian astronomer F.G.W. Struve are referred to by their

Struve numbers. Variable stars have a nomenclature all their own. Those that are not named under the existing systems are given one or two Roman letters (e.g. W Virginis, RR Lyrae). When all possible letter combinations have been used up, the variable stars in a constellation are denoted by the letter V and a number, e.g. V 1500 Cygni.

Objects such as star clusters, nebulae, and galaxies have their own systems of nomenclature, the most familiar of which are the M and NGC numbers. The M numbers come from a catalog of over 100 clusters and nebulous objects compiled in the eighteenth century by the French astronomer Charles Messier. The NGC numbers come from the *New General Catalog of Nebulae and Clusters of Stars* published in 1888 by the Danish astronomer J. L. E. Dreyer. Two supplements to the NGC, called the *Index Catalogs*, appeared in 1895 and 1908; objects listed in these are given IC numbers. Some objects have both M numbers and NGC numbers.

Star types

Stars are incandescent balls of gas, similar in nature to the Sun but so far away that they appear as nothing more than points of light in even the largest telescopes. Nevertheless, by analyzing the light from the stars, astronomers have been able to deduce that stars come in a wide range of sizes, temperatures, colors, and brightnesses. The largest stars, aptly known as *giants* and *supergiants*, are hundreds of times the diameter of the Sun, so that they would encompass the orbit of the Earth if they were placed where our Sun is. Stars of such enormous girth are at a more advanced stage of evolution than our own Sun, which itself will swell up into a red giant toward the end of its life. Supergiants differ from ordinary giants simply by being more massive. At the other end of the scale are the *red dwarf* stars that have about one-tenth the diameter of the Sun; these are stars that were born with much less mass than the Sun. Most remarkable of all are the super-dense *white dwarf* stars which have the mass of the Sun packed into a sphere the size of the Earth. These are thought to be the exposed central cores of former red giant stars whose outer layers of rarefied gas have dissipated into space.

Star colors

Not all stars are white as they at first appear. More careful inspection reveals that stars come in a wide range of colors, from deep orange through yellow to blue-white. The color of a star depends on its surface temperature, with the coolest stars being the reddest and the hottest ones the bluest. Therefore a star's color is a clue to its physical nature. The stars with the most prominent colors are the red giants such as Betelgeuse in Orion, Aldebaran in Taurus, and Antares in Scorpius. Star colors are more prominent through binoculars and telescopes than with the naked eye. Particularly attractive are double stars (p.16) in which the stars are of contrasting colors.

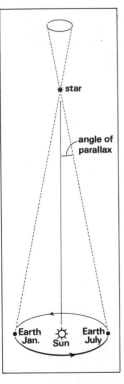

star

angle of parallax

Earth Jan.

Sun

Earth July

Parallax, a star's change in postion as seen from the opposite sides of the Earth's orbit, reveals the star's distance

Star distances

Distances between stars and galaxies are usually measured either in light years (abbreviated l.y.) or parsecs; here the *light year* is used. It is the distance that a beam of light, moving at 300,000 km per second, travels in one year. One l.y. is equivalent to 9.5 trillion km.

The distances of the nearest stars can be measured directly by a technique known as *parallax*. This involves measuring the star's precise position against the celestial background, as seen from opposite sides of the Earth's orbit. A shift in the star's position when seen from the two viewpoints (on either side of the Sun, six months apart) reveals the star's distance, with the nearest stars

13

to us showing the greatest amount of parallax shift. A star at a distance of 3.26 l.y. would show a parallax shift of one second of arc; hence a distance of 3.26 l.y. is known as a *parsec* (short for parallax of one second). In practice, no star is quite this close. The nearest star to us, α (alpha) Centauri, has a parallax of 0.76 seconds of arc, which makes its distance 4.3 l.y.

Beyond about 100 l.y. the parallaxes of stars are too small to be measured accurately by telescopes on the ground. Astronomers then have to use an indirect method that involves estimating the star's luminosity from fatures of its spectrum; they can then work out how far away from us the star must be to account for its brightness as seen in the sky. This method is open to considerable error, but it is the only technique we have for finding the distance of the majority of stars.

Variable stars

Some stars are not constant in brightness, but vary over periods of time ranging from hours to weeks or even years. The brightness of a variable star can be estimated by comparison with surrounding stars that do not vary in brightness.

The most common cause of variation is that the star actually pulsates in size as a result of an instability. A celebrated class of pulsating variables is the Cepheids, named after their prototype, δ (delta) Cephei. These are yellow supergiant stars that pulsate regularly every few days or weeks. Their importance to astronomers is that their period of pulsation is directly related to their luminosity, the brightest Cepheids taking the longest to pulsate. Consequently, by observing a Cepheid's pulsation period, astronomers can accurately ascertain its luminosity, and by comparing the luminosity with the star's brightness as it appears from Earth, they can work out how far away it is. Cepheids are thus an important tool for calibrating distances in the universe.

For all their importance, Cepheids are relatively rare. The most abundant type of variable stars are actually the red giants and supergiants, virtually all of which exhibit some form of variability due to pulsations in size, although they do not have the strict periodicity of Cepheids; a famous example of a red giant variable is o (omicron) Ceti, popularly known as Mira. Some red variable stars, such as the supergiant Betelgeuse, follow no detectable period at all.

A totally different type of variable star is the *eclipsing binary*. It consists of two stars in mutual orbit, one periodically moving in front of the other as seen from Earth. Each eclipse of one star by the other causes a dip in the total light that we receive. The most famous eclipsing binary star is Algol, also known as β (beta) Persei (see page 174).

Most spectacular of all are the eruptive variables which undergo sudden and often very large changes in light output, most notably the novae and supernovae. A *nova* is thought to be a close double star in which one member is a white dwarf. Gas from the companion star spills onto the white dwarf where it ignites explosively, causing the star's light to surge temporarily by thousands of times. The star is not destroyed in a nova explosion; some novae have been seen to erupt more than once, and possibly all novae may recur given time. Novae are often first spotted by amateur astronomers.

Even more spectacular than normal novae are the *supernovae,* celestial cataclysms that signal the death of a massive star. In a supernova, the star ends its life by blowing itself to bits, temporarily shining as brightly as billions of normal stars. Where the super nova occurred, the wreckage of the star is left to drift away into space, as with the Crab Nebula in Taurus and the Veil Nebula in Cygnus. To become a super nova, a star must have a mass several times that of our own Sun. The last supernova in our Galaxy was seen in 1604, and we are long overdue for another one.

Double and multiple stars

When examined through telescopes, many stars are found not to be single, as they appear to the naked eye, but to be accompanied by one or more companions. In some cases the stars are not really connected but simply happen to lie in the same line of sight by chance; such an arrangement is known as an *optical double.* But in the great majority of cases the stars are linked by gravity and orbit around each

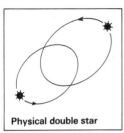

Physical double star

Optical double star

In a physical double, two stars orbvit each other; in an optica l double, the stars lie in the same line of sight.

other, the exact time taken depending on their distance apart. A pair of stars linked in this way is known as a *binary*; sometimes whole families of three or more stars, called *multiple stars*, may be interlinked by gravity.

The apparent separation of two stars in a double is measured in seconds of arc. (There are 60 seconds (") in a minute (') arc, and 60 minutes of arc in a degree (°), so that one second of arc is 1/3600th of a degree. The apparent diameter of the Moon is about 30 minutes of arc, or half a degree.) The widest doubles – those with separations of several seconds of arc or more – can be divided in small telescopes or even binoculars, but the closer together the components of a double star are, the larger the aperture of telescope needed to separate them. The steadiness of the air, known as the seeing, will also affect the ability to separate close doubles. The best examples of observable doubles are described in the text accompanying each map.

Star clusters

Stars sometimes group together in clusters, of which there are two main types: open clusters and globular clusters. *Open clusters* are the less densely packed of the two types: they are usually irregular in shape, and contain anything up to many thousands of relatively young stars. They lie in the spiral arms of our Galaxy. Famous examples are the Pleiades and Hyades clusters in Taurus, and the Double Custer in Perseus. Open clusters frequently cover half a degree of sky or more, i.e. are equal to or greater than the apparent diameter of the full Moon.

Globular clusters are dense, ball-shaped aggregations that can contain hundreds of thousands of stars. They are distributed in a halo around our Galaxy, so they are usually much further away from us than open clusters and in general they appear smaller and are more difficult to resolve into individual stars. In contrast to open clusters, globular clusters contain some of the oldest stars known. Famous examples are ω (omega) Centauri, 47 Tucanae, and M 13 in Hercules.

Nebulae

Nebulae are clouds of gas and dust in space, some of which glow brightly while others are dark. In bright nebulae, the gas and dust is lit up by the stars that lie within them. Famous examples of bright nebulae are the Orion Nebula and the Tarantula Nebula (in Dorado). By contrast, dark nebulae are visible only because they blot out light from objects behind them. One famous dark nebula is the Coalsack in Crux, the Southern Cross, which obscures part of the Milky Way star fields in that region. Some dark nebulae are seen in silhouette against bright nebulae.

Planetary nebulae

Planetary nebulae are clouds of gas that have been thrown off by a central star like the Sun at the end of its life. Their name is misleading, for planetary nebulae have nothing to do with real planets at all. Rather, the name was given because their appearance often resembles the disc of a planet, as seen through small telescopes.

Milky Way

All the stars visible to the naked eye are part of an enormous system of at least 100,000 million stars known as the Galaxy (our Galaxy is given a capital letter to distinguish it from other galaxies – see below). Those stars nearest to us in the Galaxy are scattered more or less at random across the sky and make up the constellations. The more distant ones mass into a faint band of light seen crossing the sky on clear nights. This is the Milky Way, and is shown on the constellation maps in this book as a light blue band. Sometimes the term Milky Way is used as an alternative name for our Galaxy. Our Galaxy has a spiral shape, with most of the stars and nebulae concentrated in curving arms that wind outward from a bulging central core. The Galaxy is about 100,000 l.y. in diameter and the Sun lies 30,000 l.y. from its center. The center of our Galaxy lies in the direction of the constellation Sagittarius, a region in which the Milky Way star fields are particularly dense. The entire Galaxy is rotating; our Sun takes about 250 million years to complete one orbit around the center of the Galaxy.

Galaxies

Galaxies extend into space as far as the largest telescopes can see. Each is a collection of millions or billions of stars held together by the mutual attraction of gravity. Galaxies ae classified according to their shapes, of which there are two main forms: spiral and elliptical. Spiral galaxies are sub-divided into normal spirals and barred spirals. Our own Milky Way Galaxy is a normal spiral, as is the famous neighbor and near-twin of our own, the Andromeda Galaxy. Most galaxies within reach of amateur telescopes are also normal spirals, with a central bulge of stars from which arms curve outward.

Above: a spiral galaxy, M 74 in pisces. *Below*: a barred spiral galaxy, NCG 1300 in Eridanus. *Hale Observatories*

Barred spirals differ by having a straight bar of stars across their center; the spiral arms emerge from the ends of this bar. Spiral galaxies are oriented at different angles with respect to us, which affects the way they appear in the telescope. For instance, a spiral seen face-on appears circular in telescopes, but an edge-on spiral appears cigar-shaped.

Elliptical galaxies come in a wide range of sizes, from the most massive, to the smallest galaxies of all. They are elliptical in outline and have no spiral arms. There are also a few galaxies that are irregular in shape. These include the two Magellanic Clouds, which are satellite galaxies of our Milky Way, although there is a trace of spiral form in the Large Magellanic Cloud.

Since galaxies are faint and fuzzy, they are best viewed with low magnification to increase the contrast against the sky background.

Star positions and motions

In the sky, the equivalent of longitude and latitude is right ascension (R.A.) and declination (dec.). *Right ascension* starts at the place where the Sun on its yearly path around the sky (the ecliptic) moves northward across the celestial equator. This point, known as the *vernal equinox*, is the celestial equivalent of the Greenwich meridian on Earth. Right ascension is measured eastward from the vernal equinox around the sky in hours, from 0 to 24. Each hour of right ascension is divided into 60 minutes, and each minute is divided into 60 seconds. *Declination* is measured in degrees north and south of the celestial equator, from 0 degrees at the equator to +90 degrees at the north celestial pole and −90 degrees at the south celestial pole. The celestial poles lie directly above the Earth's poles, and the celestial equator is directly overhead as seen from the Earth's equator. The position of a star or any other object can therefore be specified precisely in terms of right ascension and declination, like the coordinates of a point on Earth. Coordinate grids are overlain on each of the star maps in this book.

But celestial cartographers are faced with two problems that do not concern their terrestrial counterparts. Firstly, each star is very slowly moving relative to its neighbors; and secondly, the entire coordinate grid is itself shifting due to a wobble of the Earth in space. The movements of the stars are known as their *proper motions.* With few exceptions, e.g. Barnard's Star (see page 162), the proper motions of stars are so small as to be undetectable over a human lifetime except by precise measurements. Over many thousands of years these motions will build up until the present shapes of the constellations are totally changed, and stars will have strayed into neighboring constellations. One day, astronomers will have to revise the current nomenclature of stars and constellations.

The wobble of the Earth on its axis, called *precession,* causes the point where the ecliptic intersects the celestial equator to move once around the sky every 26,000 years. Therefore the coordinates of all points in the sky are gradually changing, and it is customary to give the coordinates of celestial objects with respect to a certain reference date. In the case of this book the reference date is the year 2000, so the star maps herein will be usable without serious error until the middle of the twenty-first century.

Planets

In addition to the fixed stars, the planets of our Solar System are also visible in the night sky. The planets shine by reflecting light from the Sun. Because they continually travel in orbit around the Sun, the planets are always moving, so they cannot be shown on the maps in this book. But when they do appear, the planets will be found near the ecliptic.

The brightest planet, Venus, outshines every star in the sky. It is frequently seen rising before the Sun in the morning sky, when it is popularly known as the morning star, or setting in the evening twilight when it is termed the evening star. A small telescope will reveal that Venus is not a star at all, for it shows a disk that goes through phases (like those of the Moon) as it orbits the Sun. The second-brightest planet is Jupiter, which at its brightest can also easily outshine any star. Unlike Venus, which keeps close to the Sun, Jupiter can be seen in any part of the sky. Even binoculars, if held steadily, reveal its four brightest moons that circle it incessantly (Io, Europa,

Ganymede, and Callisto), changing their positions from night to night.

Mars and Saturn can also feature prominently in the night sky. Mars is notable because of its glaring red color, but it is a disappointing sight in amateur telescopes because of its small size. Saturn, by contrast, is perhaps the most beautiful telescopic sight of all, being encircled by a halo of rings composed of snowballs that orbit it like a swarm of tiny moons. Of the other planets, Mercury is an elusive object, never straying far enough from the Sun to be easily visible, and Uranus, Neptune, and Pluto are distant and faint.

Meteors

Occasionally a bright streak of light will be seen darting across the sky, lasting no more than a second or so. This is a *meteor*, popularly known as a *shooting star*. Meteors have nothing to do with stars. They are actually specks of dust burning up by friction as they dash at high speed into the Earth's upper atmosphere. We do not see the speck of dust itself, but rather the trail of hot gas that it produces as it burns up at a height of about 60 mi.

On any clear night a few meteors can be seen without binoculars each hour; these random arrivals are known as *sporadic meteors*. But several times each year the Earth passes through a swarm of interplanetary dust, which gives rise to a *meteor shower*. The members of a meteor shower all appear to come from one small area of sky, known as the *radiant*. The shower is named after the constellation in which the radiant lies, e.g. the Geminids, appear to radiate from Gemini. One exception is the Quadrantids, which radiate from a part of the sky once occupied by the now-defunct constellation Quadrans Muralis, the mural quadrant, now part of Boötes. A meteor shower may last for days or even weeks as the Earth passes through the swarm of dust, but usually the peak of activity is confined to one particular night.

In the case of the richest showers, such as the Perseids in August, dozens of meteors explode along their path, becoming bright enough to cast shadows. Some meteors leave trains which slowly fade. The number of meteors in a shower is expressed in terms of the *zenithal hourly rate* (ZHR). This is the number of meteors an observer would see each hour if the radiant were directly overhead; in practice it seldom is, and so the actual number of meteors seen will be less than the ZHR. Also, if conditions are less than perfect – e.g. polluted skies or the presence of bright moonlight – then the number of meteors seen will again be reduced. The main meteor showers of the year are listed in the table opposite.

Annual meteor showers (average annual figures)

Shower	Date(s) of maximum	ZHR
Quadratids	January 3–4	100
Lyrids	April 21–22	12
η (eta) Aquarids	May 5–6	40
δ (delta) Aquarids	July 28–29	20
Perseids	August 12	60
Orionids	October 21	20
Taurids	November 3	12
Leonids	November 17–18	10
Geminids	December 13–14	60

Key to the symbols used on the constellation maps

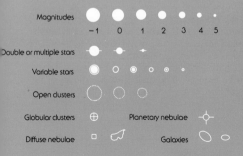

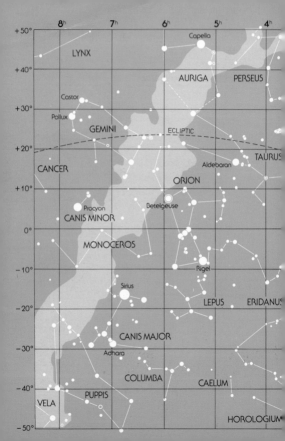

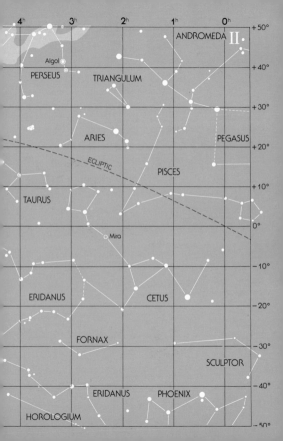

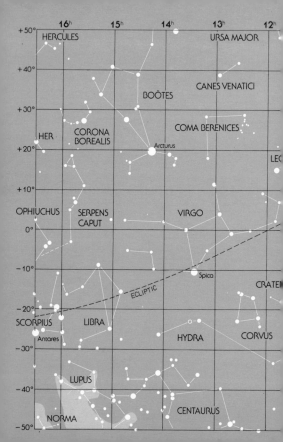

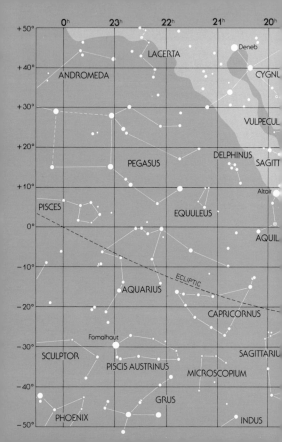

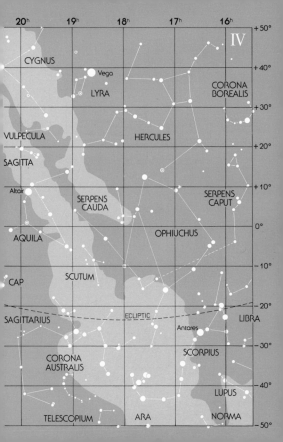

ANDROMEDA

A large constellation of the northern hemisphere of the sky, Andromeda represents the daughter of Queen Cassiopeia and King Cepheus. In Greek mythology, Andromeda was chained to a rock as a sacrifice to the sea monster Cetus, but was saved from certaindeath by the intervention of the hero Perseus.

Bright star
α (alpha) Andromedae (Sirrah or Alpheratz) is a blue-white star of mag. 2.1. Its two alternative names both come from the Arabic meaning "horse's navel", for it was once considered to be part of neighoring Pegasus. It now marks the head of Andromeda.

Double stars
γ (gamma) Andromedae is a glorious double star. Even small telescopes easily divide its two components of mags. 2.2 and 5.0. Their beautifully contrasting colors of yellow and blue make this one of the showpiece doubles of the sky.

56 And is a pair of 6th-mag. yellow giant stars, divisible in binoculars, near to the star cluster NGC 752.

Star cluster
NGC 752 is a large, scattered binocluster cluster of up to 100 stars of 9th and 10th-mag.

continued

ANDROMEDA

LACERTA

PEGASUS

+20°

+30°

23ʰ

ο

7662

+40°

ι

+50°

λ
κ

ψ

0ʰ

CASSIOPEIA

θ

ϱ

σ

α

Sirrah

π

δ

ε

ζ

η

1ʰ

205

M31

μ

ν

M32

φ

ξ

β

Mirach

PISCES

51

ω

χ

υ

τ

2ʰ

752

56

ν

TRIANGULUM

γ

Alamak

891

3ʰ

PERSEUS

Algol

ARIES

1

Galaxies

M 31 (NGC 224), the great Andromeda Galaxy, one of the most famous objects in the entire sky, is the more distant object visible to the naked eye. It is a spiral galaxy similar to our own Milky Way, but 2.2 million l.y. away. On clear, dark nights it can be seen by the naked eye as a hazy smudge; binoculars show its elliptical shape more distinctly. Only the brightest central part of the galaxy is visible through amateur instruments. Long-exposure photographs reveal the full extent of its spiral arms, which span nearly 3° of sky, i.e. six times the width of the full Moon. Also visible in small amateur telescopes is a satellite galaxy, known as M 32 or NGC 221, which appears like a fuzzy 9th-mag. star 0.5° south of M 31's core. Another satellite galaxy, NGC 205, is larger but fainter, and lies over 1° northwest of M 31.

Planetary nebula

NGC 7662 is one of the easiest planetary nebulae to see with small amateur telescopes. Under high magnfication it appears as a fuzzy blue-green disk with an elliptical outline.

The Andromeda Galaxy, M 31, with its companions M 32 (below center) and NGC 205 (upper right). Hale Observatories

ANTLIA The Air Pump

A faint and obscure constellation in the southern hemisphere of the sky, Antlia represents the pump invented by the English physicist Robert Boyle. There are no bright stars in Antlia.

Double star

ζ^1 ζ^2 (zeta^1 zeta^2) Antliae is a wide pair of 6th-mag. stars easily seen in binoculars. Small telescopes show that ζ^1 (zeta^1) Ant also has a 7th-mag. companion.

Planetary nebula

NGC 3132 on the borders with Vela is a large, bright planetary nebular of similar size to the more famous Ring Nebula in Lyra but a full magnitude brighter. In telescopes it appears as a hazy, elliptical disk larger than the apparent size of the planet Jupiter.

APUS The Bird of Paradise

An unremarkable constellation in the south polar region of the sky. It contains no bright stars.

Double star

δ^1 δ^2 (delta^1 delta^2) Apodis is a pair of 5th-mag. orange giant stars easily visible in binoculars.

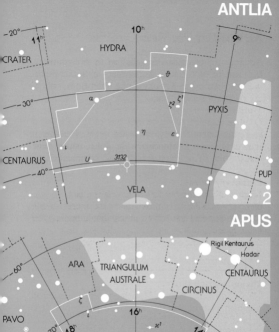

ANTLIA

CRATER
HYDRA
PYXIS
CENTAURUS
VELA
PUP

11ʰ
10ʰ
9ʰ

−20°
−30°
−40°

α
ϑ
ζ² ζ¹
ε
η
ι
U   3132

2

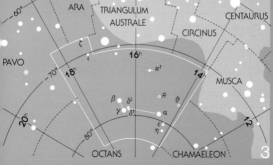

APUS

ARA
TRIANGULUM
AUSTRALE
CIRCINUS
CENTAURUS
Rigil Kentaurus
Hadar
MUSCA
PAVO
OCTANS
CHAMAELEON

−60°
−70°
−80°

16ʰ
18ʰ
20ʰ
14ʰ
12ʰ

ζ
ι
κ¹
β
δ²
γ
δ¹
R
α
ϑ
ε
η

3

AQUARIUS The Water Carrier

Aquarius is a constellation of the zodiac, through which the Sun passes from mid February to mid March. Aquarius represents a man pouring water from a jar.

Double star

ζ (zeta) Aquarii is the central star of the Y-shaped grouping that makes up the water jar of Aquarius. It is a tight pair of 4th-mag. white stars, which need telescopes of at least 75mm aperture and high magnification to be divided.

Globular clusters

M 2 (NGC 7089) is a rich globular cluster of 6th mag. It appears as a hazy patch in binoculars and small telescopes.

M 72 (NGC 6981) is a 9th-mag. globular cluster, unimpressive in small telescopes.

Planetary nebulae

NGC 7009, the Saturn Nebula, appears as a small greenish disk of 8th mag. in small telescopes. It is named the Saturn Nebula because in large telescopes its shape resembles that of the planet Saturn.

NGC 7293, the Helix Nebula, is the closest planetary nebula to us, about 600 l.y. away, and the largest in apparent size. Its diameter is 16' of arc, half that of the Moon. Although large it is faint, and is best seen

continued

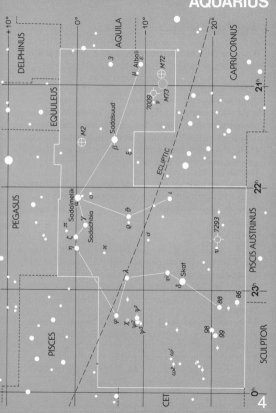

AQUARIUS

DELPHINUS

+10°

0°

AQUILA

−10°

−20°

CAPRICORNUS

3

μ Albali ε

M72

21ʰ

EQUULEUS

7009 ν M73

Sadalsuud

M2

β ξ

ECLIPTIC

22ʰ

PEGASUS

Sadalmelik α ο

ι

γ θ ρ

Sadachbia κ σ

ν 7293

PISCIS AUSTRINUS

η ζ π

λ

τ

δ Skat

23ʰ

PISCES

φ χ ψ¹ ψ² ψ³

88

86

98

99

ω² ω¹

SCULPTOR

CET

0ʰ

4

AQUILA The Eagle

A constellation straddling the celestial equator, Aquila represents an eagle.

Bright star

α (alpha) Aquilae (Altair, Arabic for flying eagle) is a white star of mag. 0.8. It forms one corner of the so-called Summer Triangle of stars, the other two being Deneb in Cygnus and Vega in Lyra. Altair is 16 l.y. away, one of the closest stars to us.

Variable star

η (eta) Aquilae is one of the brightest Cepheid variables, ranging from mag. 4.1 to mag. 5.3 every 7.2 days. *continued*

Aquarius continued

in binoculars, or telescopes with low magnification, which show it as a circular misty patch. Its full beauty is brought out in long-exposure photographs, where it appears like two overlapping loops of gas.

Meteors

Three meteor showers radiate from Aquarius each year. The richest shower, the η (eta) Aquarids, reach a maximum of about 40 per hour on May 5; the δ (delta) Aquarids produce about 20 meteors per hour around July 28; and on August 6 the ι (iota) Aquarids reach about 8 meteors per hour.

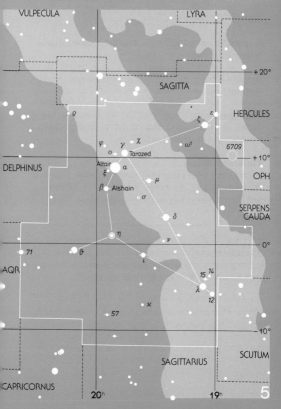

AQUILA

VULPECULA

LYRA

SAGITTA

HERCULES

ζ   ε

ω¹

6709

+20°

φ   γ   χ

o   Tarazed

Altair

ξ   α

β   Alshain

μ

σ

δ

+10°

DELPHINUS

OPH

SERPENS
CAUDA

ϱ

η

ϑ

ν

0°

71

ι

AQR

15 14

λ

12

ϰ

57

δ

-10°

SAGITTARIUS

SCUTUM

CAPRICORNUS

20ʰ

19ʰ

5

ARA The Altar

A small constellation of the southern celestial hemisphere, Ara is visualized by the Greeks as the altar on which Centaurus the centaur was about to sacrifice Lupus the wolf. It has no stars brighter than 3rd mag.

Star cluster
NGC 6193 is a binocular cluster of about 30 stars, the brightest of which is of 6th mag.

Globular cluster
NGC 6397 is possibly the closest globular cluster to us, about 7500 l.y. away. It appears as a 7th-mag. smudge in binoculars and small telescopes.

Aquila continued

Double stars
15 Aquilae is a 5th-mag. yellow star with a 7th-mag. companion easily visible in small telescopes.

57 Aquilae is an easy pair of 6th mag. stars for small telescopes.

ARA

SAGITTARIUS

SCORPIUS

LUPUS

—40°

CORONA
AUSTRALIS

σ
ι
λ α ⊕ 6352   6193
ϑ
—50°
μ
κ
6397 ⊕   ε² ε¹
TELESCOPIUM
π
β
γ   ζ
NORMA
η

—60°
δ

PAVO   ⊕ 6362   TRIANGULUM
AUSTRALE

—70°   CIR
18ʰ   17ʰ
19ʰ   16ʰ
20ʰ   15ʰ
OCTANS   APUS

6

ARIES The Ram

An important constellation of the zodiac, the Sun is in Aries from late April to mid-May. Aries represents the ram whose golden fleece was sought by Jason and the Argonauts. The importance of Aries lies in the fact that it once contained the vernal equinox, i.e. the point where the Sun crosses the celestial equator moving from south to north; this is the zero point of right ascension, the celestial equivalent of the Greenwich meridian. The effect of procession has now moved the vernal equinox into neighboring Pisces, but for historical reasons the vernal equinox is still referred to as the First Point of Aries.

Bright star
α (alpha) Arietis (Hamal, from the Arabic for sheep) is a yellow giant of mag. 2.0.

Double stars
γ (gamma) Arietis is an easy pair for small telescopes, consisting of two white stars of 5th mag.

λ (lambda) Aries is a 5th-mag. white star with a 7th-mag. companion visible in binoculars or small telescopes.

π (pi) Arietis, a blue-white 5th-mag. star, has a close 8th-mag. companion visible in small telescopes under high magnification.

ARIES

PISCES

+ 30°

+ 20°

+ 10°

ANDROMEDA

Mesarthim

Sheratan

β

γ

ι

λ

α

κ

Hamal

η

ECLIPTIC

ξ

TRIANGULUM

ν

π

σ

CETUS

41

ε

ζ

δ

τ

PLEIADES

Pleiades

TAURUS

2ʰ

3ʰ

4ʰ

PERSEUS

7

AURIGA The Charioteer

Auriga is a large constellation of the northern hemisphere of the sky. γ (gamma) Aurigae is shared with Taurus and is dealt with under that constellation as β (beta) Tauri.

Bright star

α (alpha) Aurigae (Capella), mag. 0.1, is the 6th-brightest star in the entire sky. It is a yellow giant 42.1 l.y. away.

Variable star

ε (epsilon) Aurigae is an eclipsing binary of exceptionally long period. Every 27 years it sinks from mag. 3.0 to 3.8 as it is eclipsed by a dark companion; the eclipses last for a full year. Its last eclipse was in 1983.

Double stars

θ (theta) Aurigae is a tight double of mag. 2.6 with a 7th-mag. companion requiring a telescope with at least 100 mm aperture and high magnification to distinguish.

ω (omega) Aurigae is a double star for small telescopes consisting of stars of 5th and 8th mags.

Star clusters

M 36 (NGC 1960) is a binocular cluster of 60 stars.

continued

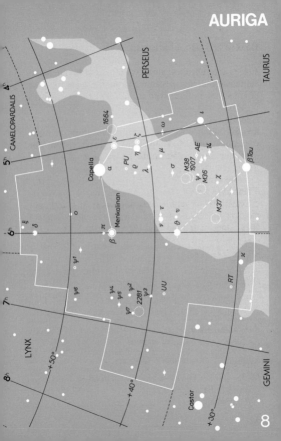

BOÖTES The Herdsman

A large constellation of the northern celestial hemisphere, Boötes represents a man driving the bear of Ursa Major around the sky.

Bright star

α (alpha) Boötis (Arcturus, from the Greek for bear-keeper), mag. 0.0, is the 4th-brightest star in the entire sky. It is a red giant 36.1 l.y. away.

Double stars

ε (epsilon) Boötis (Izar of Pulcherrima) is a glorious but difficult pair with contrasting colors of orange and blue, of 3rd and 5th mag. Their closeness requires atleast 75 mm aperture and high power to split.

μ (mu) Boötis, a blue-white star of 4th mag., has a 7th-mag. binocular companion. The companion is itself double, as revealed under high power by telescopes of at least 75 mm aperture.

continued

Auriga continued

M 37 (NGC 2099) is the richest of the clusters in Auriga. It contains about 150 stars.

M 38 (NGC 1912) is a large, scattered binocular cluster of about 100 stars. Next to it lies NGC 1907, a much smaller and fainter cluster.

BOÖTES

DRACO

URSA MAJOR

HERCULES

CANES VENATICI

44

ϑ κ ι

λ

φ ν^2 ν^1

β Nekkar

Alkalurops

μ

γ Haris

CORONA BOREALIS

δ

χ

ϱ

ψ

σ

ε Izar

ω

W

COMA BERENICES

ξ

η

o

α Arcturus

τ

π

υ

SERPENS CAPUT

ζ

VIRGO

9

16^h 15^h 14^h 13^h

+50°

+40°

+30°

+20°

+10°

CAELUM The Chisel

A faint and easily overlooked constellation of the southern sky, Caelum's brightest star is of mag. 4.5.

Double star

γ (gamma) Caeli is a pair of 5th and 8th mag. stars for small telescopes.

Boötes continued

ν¹ ν² (nu¹ nu²) Boötis area wide pair of unrelated white and orange 5th-mag. stars.

ξ (xi) Boötis is a beautiful duo for small telescopes, consisting of a yellow and an orange star of 5th and 7th mags.

Meteors

The Quadrantids, the year's most abundant meteor shower, radiate from the northern part of Boötes, reaching a maximum of about 100 meteors per hour on January 3–4. The shower takes its name from a now-abandoned constellation, Quadrans Muralis, the Mural Quadrant, that once occupied this area of sky. Although they are plentiful, the Quadrantids are not as bright as other great showers such as the Perseids.

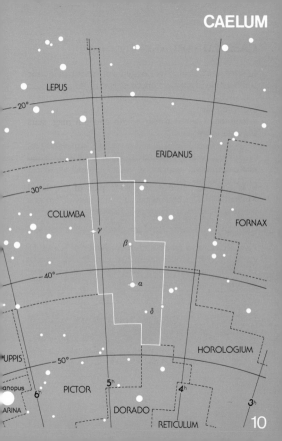

CAELUM

LEPUS

−20°

ERIDANUS

COLUMBA

−30°

FORNAX

γ

β

−40°

α

δ

HOROLOGIUM

UPPIS

−50°

anopus

PICTOR

6ʰ

ARINA

5ʰ

4ʰ

3ʰ

DORADO

RETICULUM

10

CAMELOPARDALIS The Giraffe

Camelopardalis is a large but inconspicuous constellation in the north polar region of the sky, which also used to be called Camelopardus. Its brightest stars are of 4th mag.

Double stars

β (beta) Camelopardalis is a yellow supergiant of mag. 4.0, the brightest star in the constellation; it has a wide 9th-mag. companion visible in small telescopes and good binoculars.

Struve 1694 (Σ 1694) is an attractive pair of 5th and 6th mag. white stars easily split in small telescopes.

Star cluster

NGC 1502 is a small binocular cluster of about 15 stars. Small telescopes reveal two easy double stars at its center, one pair of 6th mag. and the other pair of 9th mag.

Galaxy

NGC 2403 is a 9th-mag. spiral galaxy visible in binoculars under good conditions.

CAMELOPARDALIS

URSA MINOR

DRACO

DRACO

Σ1694

URSA MAJOR

+90° Polaris

VZ

CEPHEUS

CASSIOPEIA

2403

γ

LYNX

α

1502

β

7

PERSEUS

AURIGA

11

CANCER The Crab

Cancer is a constellation of the zodiac, inside whose boundaries the Sun lies from late July to early August. The constellation represents the crab that attacked Hercules during his fight with Hydra, the water snake. In times past, the Sun used to lie in Cancer when at its farthest north of the celestial equator; this is the time of the summer solstice, June 21 each year. The latitude at which the Sun appears overhead when farthest north came to be known as the Tropic of Cancer. However, because of the effect of precession, the Sun now lies in neighboring Gemini on the summer solstice.

Double stars

ζ (zeta) Cancri is an attractive pair of yellow stars of 5th and 6th mags. visible through small telescopes.

ι (iota) Cancri is a 4th-mag. yellow giant with a 7th-mag. companion easily seen with small telescopes.

Star cluster

M 44 (NGC 2632) Praesepe, also popularly termed the Beehive Cluster, is a large swarm of 75 or more stars of 6th mag. and fainter. To the naked eye it appears as a musty patch. It is best seen in binoculars because of its great size, covering 1.5° of sky, three times the apparent width of the full Moon.

CANES VENATICI The Hunting Dogs

A constellation of the northern hemisphere of the sky, Canes Venatici represent the two dogs of Boötes, the herdsman.

Double star

α (alpha) Canum Venaticorum is known as Cor Caroli, meaning Charles's Heart, a name given by Edmond Halley in honor of Charles II of England. It is a blue-white star of mag. 2.9 with a 5th-mag. companion easily seen in small telescopes.

Globular cluster

M 3 (NGC 5272), of 6th mag., is visible as a hazy patch in binoculars. Although telescopes of 100mm are needed to resolve individual stars, smaller telescopes show it as a softly glowing ball of light.

Galaxies

M 51 (NGC 5194) is the famous Whirlpool Galaxy, a spiral with a satellite galaxy, NGC 5195, at the end of one of its arms. Large telescopes are needed to show it to effect; in small telescopes it appears as a hazy patch with starlike points marking the nuclei of the main galaxy and its satellite.

M 94 (NGC 4736) is an 8th-mag. spiral galaxy seen head-on, looking like a small comet in amateur telescopes.

CANES VENATICI

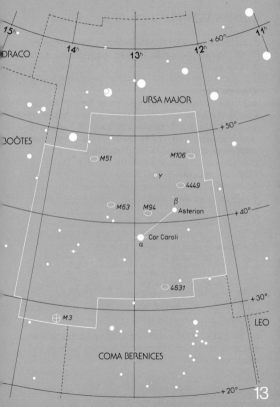

DRACO

URSA MAJOR

BOÖTES

M51

M106

γ

4449

M63   M94   β

Asterion

Cor Caroli

α

4631

LEO

M3

COMA BERENICES

13

CANIS MAJOR The Greater Dog

A compact constellation in the southern hemisphere of the sky, Canis Major contains many bright stars, notably Sirius, the brightest star of all. It represents one of the dogs of Orion, the other being represented by Canis Minor.

Bright stars

α (alpha) Canis Majoris (Sirius, from the Greek for sparkling or scorching) is the brightest star in the entire sky, of mag. −1.5. It is a white star 8.7 l.y. away, one of the closest stars to the Sun. It has an 8th-mag. white dwarf companion visible only in large amateur telecopes.

β (beta) Canis Majoris (Mirzam, the announcer, i.e. of Sirius) is a blue giant of mag. 2.0.

δ (delta) Canis Majoris (Wezen) is a yellow supergiant of mag. 1.9, 3000 l.y. away.

ε (epsilon) Canis Majoris (Adhara, the virgins), mag. 1.5, is a blue giant with an 8th-mag. companion, difficult to see in small telescopes because of the glare from the main star.

Star cluster

M 41 (NGC 2287) is a large, bright cluster whose brightest star is of 7th mag. It is just visible to the naked eye and is well seen in binoculars and small
continued

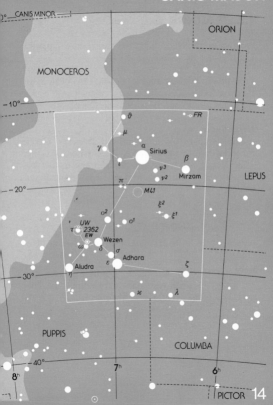

CANIS MAJOR

ORION

MONOCEROS

−10°

ϑ

μ

FR

γ

α   Sirius

ι

β

ν³

ν²   Mirzam

LEPUS

π

−20°

M41

ξ²

ξ¹

o²

o¹

UW

2362

τ   EW

ω   δ

σ   Adhara

Wezen

ε

Aludra

η

ζ

−30°

κ

λ

PUPPIS

COLUMBA

−40°

8ʰ

7ʰ

6ʰ

PICTOR   **14**

CANIS MINOR The Lesser Dog

A small constellation lying on the celestial equator, Canis Minor represents the smaller of the two dogs of Orion, Canis Major being the larger. Apart from Procyon, its brightest star, it contains little of interest. Procyon forms a triangle of brilliant stars with Sirius (in Canis Major) and Betelgeuse (in Orion).

Bright star
α (alpha) Canis Minoris (Procyon, from the Greek meaning before the dog, i.e. it rises before Canis Major), mag. 0.4, is the 8th-brightest star in the sky. It is a yellow-white star 11.3 l.y. away, one of the nearest stars to the Sun.

Canis Major continued

telescopes. Its brightest stars seem to be arranged in chains.

NGC 2362 is a cluster of about 40 stars for binoculars or small telescopes, surrounding the 4th-mag. blue giant τ (tau) Canis Majoris.

CANIS MINOR

Pollux

GEMINI

CANCER

ECLIPTIC

+20°

+10°

γ ε
Gomeisa β
η
Procyon α

ζ · δ¹

0°

HYDRA

MONOCEROS

-10°

CANIS MAJOR

PUPPIS

8ʰ

7ʰ Sirius

15

CAPRICORNUS The Sea Goat

A constellation of the zodiac, through which the Sun passes from late January to mid-February, Capricornus represents a goat with a fish tail. In ancient times the Sun lay in Capricornus at the winter solstice, its farthest point south of the equator. The effect of precession has now moved the winter solstice into neighboring Sagittarius, but the latitude on Earth at which the Sun appears overhead on that day is still known as the Tropic of Capricorn.

Double stars
α (alpha) Capricorni (Algedi, from the Arabic meaning goat or ibex) is a naked-eye pair of unrelated 4th-mag. stars. Each star is itself double. Small telescopes show that $α^1$ (alpha^1) Capricorni has a 9th-mag. companion, and $α^2$ (alpha^2) Capricorni has an 11th-mag. companion.

β (beta) Capricorni is a 3rd-mag. star with a 6th-mag. companion for binoculars or small telescopes.

Globular cluster
M 30 (NGC 7099) is an 8th-mag. globular cluster next to the 5th-mag. star, 41 Capricorni.

CAPRICORNUS

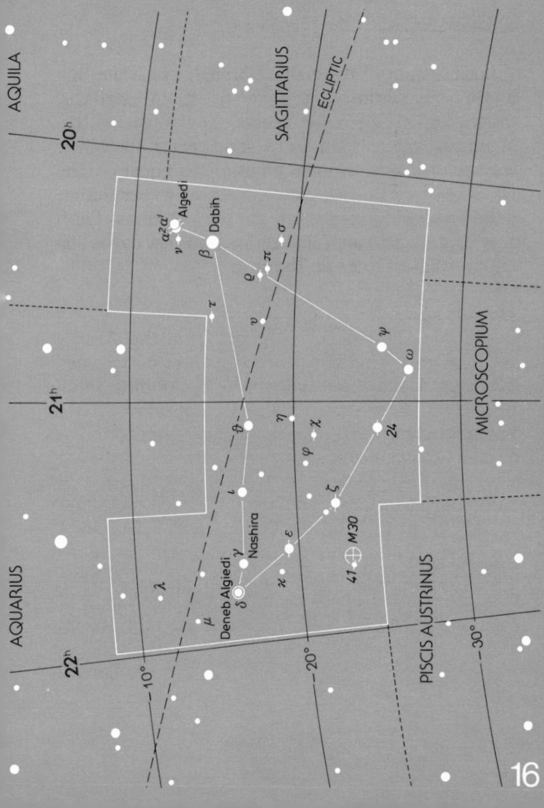

AQUILA

SAGITTARIUS

ECLIPTIC

20h

AQUARIUS

21h

MICROSCOPIUM

22h

PISCIS AUSTRINUS

ν α² α¹ Algedi
Dabih
β
π σ
ϱ
τ
ψ
ψ
ω
θ
η
χ
φ
24
ν
ζ
λ
ε
41 M30
μ
κ
γ Nashira
δ Deneb Algiedi

-10°
-20°
-30°

16

CARINA The Keel

A large constellation of the southern celestial hemisphere, Carina is one of the parts into which the constellation of Argo Navis, the ship of the Argonauts, was divided. It lies in an area of the Milky Way rich with clusters and nebulae.

Bright stars

α (alpha) Carinae (Canopus), mag. −0.7, is the second-brightest star in the sky. It is a yellow-white supergiant about 300 l.y. away.

β (beta) Carinae (Miaplacidus) is a blue-white star of mag. 1.7.

ε (epsilon) Carinae is a yellow giant star of mag. 1.9.

Variable star

η (eta) Carinae is one of the most erratically behaved stars in the heavens. In 1843 it flared up to a maximum of mag. −1, but has now settled to around 6th or 7th mag. It lies inside thenebula NGC 3372 (see page 73). η (eta) Carinae is thought to be an unstable supergiant star with a mass of over 100 Suns that throws off shells of gas at irregular intervals. It is expected to become a supernova in the next 10,000 years.

continued

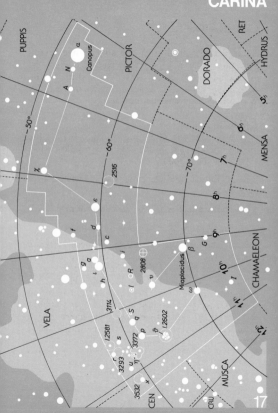

CARINA

PUPPIS

PICTOR

RET

HYDRUS

DORADO

MENSA

CHAMAELEON

VELA

MUSCA

CEN

CRU

Canopus

α
N
A

χ
2516
ε
f
d
c
i
a
g
ι
h

2808
R
I
v
Miaplacidus
β
G
ω

2602
2581
3114
q
S
p
s
r
u
T
3372
3293
3532

Myaplacidus

5ʰ
6ʰ
7ʰ
8ʰ
9ʰ
10ʰ

-50°
-60°
-70°

17

Carina continued

Double star

υ (upsilon) Carinae is a 3rd-mag. white star with a 6th-mag. companion visible in small telescopes.

Star clusters

IC 2601 is a large and bright cluster similar to the Pleiades, centered on the 3rd-mag., blue-white star O (theta) Carinae. It contains six naked-eye stars, and many more are visible in binoculars and small telescopes covering over 1° of sky.

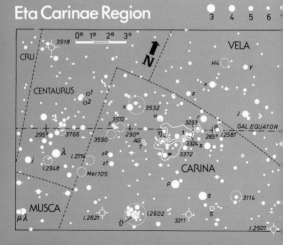

NGC 2516 is a large binocular cluster of about 100 stars, containing a 5th-mag. red giant and three double stars of 8th and 9th mags. for small telescopes.

NGC 3532 is a large binocular cluster of 150 stars of 6th mag. and fainter, which appears very rich in small telescopes which show its markedly elliptical shape. A 4th-mag. orange star at one edge is apparently not a member of the cluster, but is much more distant.

Nebula

NGC 3372, the η (eta) Carinae Nebula, is a diffuses nebula visible to the naked eye, larger than the Orion Nebula. It is bisected by a dark V-shaped lane of dust. NGC 3372 contains the erratic variable star η (eta) Carinae, which lies in the bright central part of the nebula near to a dark notch called the Keyhole because of its shape. This is a star-studded region for gazing with binoculars (see opposite).

CASSIOPEIA

A distinctive W-shaped constellation of the northern hemisphere of the sky, Cassiopeia represents a mythical Queen of Ethiopia, wife of King Cepheus and mother of Andromeda.

Variable star

γ (gamma) Cassiopeiae is an unstable blue giant that throws off shells of gas at irregular intervals, causing it to vary unpredictably between 2nd and 3rd mags.

Double and multiple stars

η (eta) Cassiopeiae is a beautiful double star for small telescopes consisting of yellow and red components of 4th and 8th mags.

ι (iota) Cassiopeiae is a 5th-mag. white star with an 8th-mag. companion divisible in small telescopes. The brighter star has a close 7th-mag. yellow companion visible with a 100mm aperture and high magnification telescope.

Star clusters

M 52 (NGC 7654) is a binocular cluster of over 100 stars, somewhat kidney-shaped and with a prominent 8th-mag. orange star at one edge.

NGC 457 is an attractive cluster for small telescopes, including the 5th-mag. yellow supergiant φ (phi) Cassiopeiae. The stars of NGC 457 are seemingly arranged in chains.

CASSIOPEIA

DRACO

CEPHEUS

CYGNUS

LACERTA

ANDROMEDA

CAMELOPARDALIS

PERSEUS

M52
7635
AR
τ
ρ
σ
R
β
Caph
Schedar
λ
α
ζ
ξ
ο
π
κ
γ
η
ν
μ
ψ
ν²
ε
ψ
RU
559
637
M103
δ
457
φ
θ
χ
663
ω
50
ι
1027
I.1805

Algol

18

CENTAURUS The Centaur

A resplendent constellation of the southern celestial hemisphere, Centaurus represents the mythical beast known as a centaur. It contains the closest known star to the Sun, α (alpha) Centauri, which is actually a triple system.

Bright stars

α (alpha) Centauri (Rigil Kentaurus, from the Arabic meaning foot of the centaur) appears to the naked eye as a star of mag. −0.3, the third-brightest in the sky. Small telescopes split it into a pair of yellow stars of mags. 0.0 and 1.4 which orbit each other every 80 years. These two stars lie 4.3 l.y. away from us. About 0.1 l.y. closer is an 11th-mag. red dwarf called Proxima Centauri; this is strictly the closest star of all to us. Proxima Centauri lies 2° away in the sky from its two brighter companions, not even in the same telescope field of view.

β (beta) Centauri (Hadar or Agena) is a blue giant of mag. 0.6, the 11th-brightest star in the sky. A line drawn from α (alpha) through β (beta) Centauri points to Crux, the Southern Cross.

Double star

3 Centauri (also known as k Centauri) is a neat pair of blue-white stars of 5th and 6th mags. for small telescopes.

continued

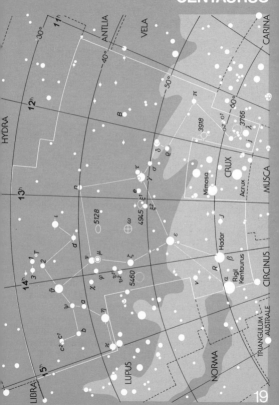

Planetary nebula

NGC 3918 is an 8th-mag. planetary nebula with a small blue-green disk similar in appearance to the planet Uranus. John Herschel called this the Blue Planetary.

Globular cluster

ω (omega) Centauri (NGC 5139) is the largest and brightest globular cluster in the sky, covering a larger area than the full Moon. To the naked eye it appears as a fuzzy 4th-mag. star, somewhat elliptical in outline. Small telescopes or even binoculars begin to resolve its outer regions into a granular mass of sparkling stars. It is one of the closest globulars to us, about 16,000 l.y. away.

Galaxy

NGC 5128 is a peculiar galaxy also known as the radio source Centaurus A, visible in binoculars or small telescopes as a 7th-mag. hazy blur. Long-exposure photographs show that it is a giant elliptical galaxy crossed by a band of dark dust. One possibility is that we are seeing an elliptical galaxy merging with a spiral galaxy, the spiral galaxy providing the lane of dust. It is one of the strongest sources known to radio astronomers, who have detected lobes of radio emission either side of the galaxy, as though it has ejected clouds of gas in a series of explosions. It lies about 15 million l.y. away.

The enormous radio galaxy NGC 5128, also known as centaurus A, can be seen in small telescopes. *Hale Observatories*

CEPHEUS

A constellation of the north polar region of the sky, Cepheus represents a mythical King of Ethiopia, husband of Queen Cassiopeia and father of Andromeda. It contains the celebrated variable star δ (delta) Cephei.

Variable stars

δ (delta) Cephei is the prototype of the most important type of variable stars known to astronomers, the Cepheid variables. Thanks to the so-called Period-Luminosity Law, astronomers can derive a Cepheid's absolute magnitude by observing its period of variation; Cepheid variables are therefore the "standard candles" by which astronomers measure distances in space. The variability of δ (delta) Cephei was discovered in 1784 by the English amateur astronomer John Goodricke. δ (delta) Cephei is a yellow supergiant that varies between mags. 3.6 and 4.3 every 5 days 9 hours. δ (delta) Cephei is also a double star (see following page).

μ (mu) Cephei is a red supergiant, prototype of the class of semiregular variables. It varies between mags. 3.6 and 5.1 with no set period. Sir William Herschel named it the Garnet Star on account of its pronounced coloration: it is one of the reddest stars visible to the naked eye.

continued

CEPHEUS

CAMELOPARDALIS

URSA MINOR

+90°
Polaris

16ʰ

4ʰ

2ʰ

18ʰ

0ʰ
+80°

20ʰ

22ʰ

DRACO

γ Er Rai

ϱ

κ

π

+70°

Alfirk
β

τ

o

θ

ι

η

ξ

VV
7160

Alderamin
α

+60°

ν

CASSIOPEIA

δ

λ

μ

ζ

I.1396

ε

+50°

LACERTA

CYGNUS

ANDROMEDA

20

Double stars

β (beta) Cephei is a blue giant of 3rd mag. with an 8th-mag. companion visible in small telescopes. β (beta) Cephei is also a variable star, though its fluctuations are too small to be noticed with the naked eye, less than 0.1 mag. every 4.5 hours. It is the prototype of a class of pulsating variable stars (also known as β (beta) Canis Majoris stars) with periods of a few hours and small changes in light output.

δ (delta) Cephei, in addition to being a noted variable star (see page 00 and comparison chart opposite), is an attractive double star for small telescopes or even binoculars. The brighter cream-colored component, which is the variable, is accompanied by a wide 6th-mag. blue-white star.

ζ (xi) Cephie is a double star for small telescopes consisting of a blue-white star of 5th mag. with a 7th-mag. yellowish companion.

o (omicron) Cephei is a 5th-mag. yellow giant with a close 7th-mag. companion visible in telescopes with apertures of 60mm and above with high magnification.

δ Cephei

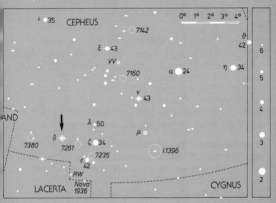

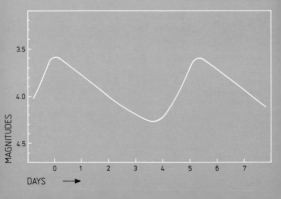

CETUS The Whale

A large constellation straddling the celestial equator, Cetus represents the sea monster that nearly devoured Andromeda before her rescue by Perseus.

Nearby star

τ (tau) Ceti is a 3rd-mag. yellow dwarf, 11.7 l.y. away. Of all the nearby single stars, this one is most similar to our own Sun.

Variable star

o (omicron) Ceti (Mira, the wonderful), a red giant, is the prototype of the long-period variables. Mira fluctuates between 3rd and 9th mags. with an average period of 330 days. Its variability was first noticed in 1596 by the Dutch astronomer David Fabricius.

Double stars

α (alpha) Ceti (Menkar, from the Arabic for nose) is a red giant of 2nd mag. with an unrelated blue 6th-mag. companion visible in binoculars.

γ (gamma) Ceti (Kaffaljidhmah) is a close pair of 4th and 6th-mag. stars requiring at least 60mm aperture and high power to split.

continued

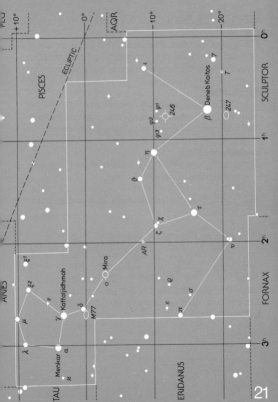

CETUS

PISCES

ECLIPTIC

AQR

SCULPTOR

+10°

0°

−10°

−20°

0ʰ

ι

Deneb Kaitos

7

τ

φ¹

246

β

247

φ²

φ³

1ʰ

η

θ

τ

χ

ζ

ʋ

AR

2ʰ

ξ¹

ξ²

ο Mira

ν

Kaffaljidhmah

δ

ϱ

γ

M77

σ

μ

ε

π

λ

α

Menkar

ϰ

ARIES

TAU

FORNAX

ERIDANUS

3ʰ

21

CHAMAELEON The Chameleon

An insignificant constellation in the south polar region of the sky, Chamaeleon represents a chameleon. Its brightest stars are of 4th mag.

Double star

δ (delta) Chamaeleontis is a binocular pair of blue and orange stars of 4th and 5th matgs. They are unrelated, lying in the same line of sight by chance.

Planetary nebula

NGC 3195 is a planetary nebula of similar apparent size to the planet Jupiter.

Cetus continued

Galaxy

M 77 (NGC 1068) is a 9th-mag. spiral galaxy presented face on. It is unimpressive in small telescopes, but its main interest is that it is the brightest of the so-called Seyfert galaxies, spiral galaxies with bright centers that are closely related to quasars. (Quasars are intensely luminous stars far off in the universe.)

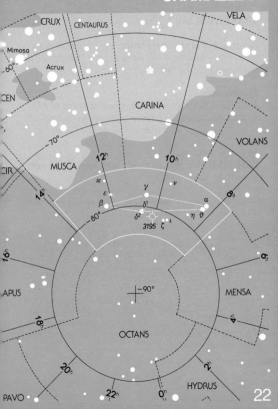

CHAMAELEON

VELA

CRUX   CENTAURUS

Mimosa

60°

Acrux

CEN

CARINA

CIR

70°

MUSCA 12ʰ 10ʰ

VOLANS

14ʰ

ϰ

ε
β

80°

γ ν

δ¹

α

η ϑ

δ² ⊙ ι ζ
3195

6ʰ

16ʰ

APUS

MENSA

18ʰ

90°

4ʰ

OCTANS

20ʰ

22ʰ 0ʰ

HYDRUS

PAVO

22

CIRCINUS The Compasses

Circinus is a small and obscure constellation of the southern hemisphere of the sky, overshadowed by neighboring Centaurus.

Double star

α (alpha) Circini is a 3rd-mag. white star with a wide 9th-mag. companion visible in small telescopes.

COLUMBA The Dove

A constellation of the southern hemisphere of the sky, Columba is usually envisaged as a dove following along after Noah's Ark. It contains no objects of interest to amateur observers.

Runaway star

μ (mu) Columbae, a 5th-mag. blue star, is one of three so-called runaway stars that seem to be diverging from a point in Orion at speeds of around 100 km/sec. The other two stars are 53 Arietis and AE Aurigae. According to one theory, the stars were once members of a quadruple system, the fourth member of which exploded as a supernova about three million years ago.

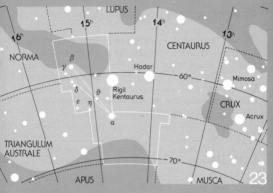

CIRCINUS

LUPUS

16ʰ

NORMA

15ʰ

14ʰ

CENTAURUS

13ʰ

β
γ

δ
ε θ
η

Rigil
Kentaurus

α

Hadar

60°

Mimosa

CRUX

Acrux

TRIANGULUM
AUSTRALE

APUS

70°

MUSCA

23

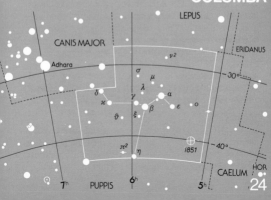

COLUMBA

LEPUS

CANIS MAJOR

Adhara

ERIDANUS

ν²

σ μ
λ
γ α
β ε ο
ξ

30°

δ
κ

θ

π² η

⊕
1851

40°

7ʰ

PUPPIS

6ʰ

5ʰ

CAELUM HOR

24

COMA BERENICES Berenice's Hair

A faint constellation of the northern sky, Coma Berenices represents the locks of the Egyptian Queen Berenice which she offered to the gods for the return of her husband from battle. Coma Berenices contains a number of galaxies within range of amateur telescopes; these are members of the Virgo Cluster that have spilled over the border.

Double star
24 Comae Berenicis, a 5th-mag. orange giant, makes a beautiful color contrast with a 7th-mag. blue-white companion, visible in small telescopes.

Star cluster
The Coma Star Cluster consists of a scattered group of about 30 stars representing Queen Berenice's severed tresses. They form a V-shaped binocular group to the south of γ (gamma) Comae Berenicis. The brightest members are of 5th and 6th mag.

Globular cluster
M 53 (NGC 5024) is an 8th-mag. globular cluster, visible as a misty patch in small telescopes.

Galaxy
M 64 (NGC 4826) is a 9th-mag. spiral galaxy visible in small telescopes. It is popularly called the Black Eye Galaxy because of a dark patch of dust near its center, shown by telescopes of 150mm and above.

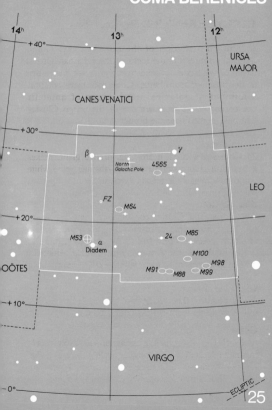

14ʰ

13ʰ

12ʰ

+ 40°

URSA
MAJOR

CANES VENATICI

+ 30°

β

North
Galactic Pole

γ

4565

LEO

FZ

+ 20°

M64

M53 ⊕ α
      Diadem

24

M85

OÖTES

M100

M98

M91

M88

M99

+ 10°

VIRGO

0°

ECLIPTIC

25

CORONA AUSTRALIS
The Southern Crown

A small constellation of the southern hemisphere of the sky, Corona Australis lies between Sagittarius and Scorpius. Corona Australis has been known since Greek times, and is said in legends to represent the crown worn by the neighboring centaur, Sagittarius. Despite its small size it is not without interest, lying on the edge of the Milky Way.

Double stars

γ (gamma) Coronae Australis is a tight pair of 5th-mag. yellow stars requiring at least 100mm aperture and high magnification to split.

κ (kappa) Coronae Australis is a wide pair of 6th-mag. blue-white stars easily divided by small telescopes.

λ (lambda) Coronae Australis is a 5th-mag. white star with a wide 9th-mag. companion easily seen in small telescopes.

Globular cluster

NGC 6541 is a 6th-mag. globular cluster, 14,000 l.y. away, for binoculars and small telescopes.

CORONA AUSTRALIS

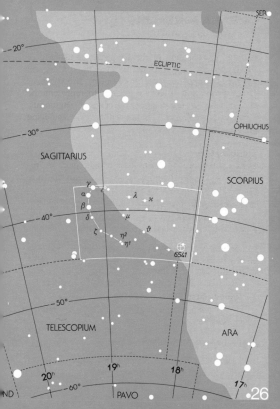

SER

ECLIPTIC

−20°

OPHIUCHUS

−30°

SAGITTARIUS

SCORPIUS

γ
α ε
β   λ   κ
δ   μ
ζ   η²   ϑ
η¹   6541

−40°

TELESCOPIUM

−50°

ARA

PAVO

20ʰ   19ʰ   18ʰ   17ʰ

−60°

ND

26

CORONA BOREALIS
The Northern Crown

A small constellation of the northern hemisphere of the sky, Corona Borealis's most feature is a crescent-shaped group of stars in which the constellation's brightest star, mag. 2.2 Gemma (also known as Alphecca), is set like a jewel in the crown.

Variable stars
R Coronae Borealis is a celebrated variable star given to catastrophic changes in brightness at intervals of a few years. Normally it is of 6th mag. but it can unpredictably drop in a few weeks to as low as 14th mag., subsequently taking some months to return to its former brightness. Its variation is thought to be due to sooty carbon particles in its outer layers, which periodically build up and then blow away.

T Coronae Borealis, known as the Blaze Star, is a recurrent nova that normally hovers around 10th mag. but which in 1866 and 1946 brightened to 2nd and 3rd mags. respectively. Further eruptions may be expected at any time.

Double stars
ζ (zeta) Coronae Borealis is a pair of 5th and 6th-mag. blue stars for small telescopes.

v^1 v^2 (nu^1 nu^2) Coronae Borealis is a wide binocular pair of unrelated 5th-mag. orange giants.

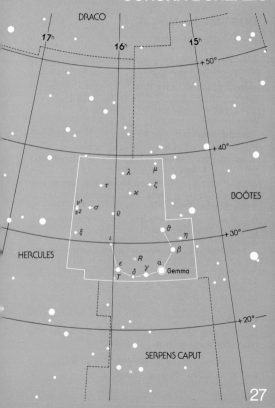

DRACO

17ʰ

16ʰ

15ʰ

+50°

+40°

BOÖTES

λ

μ

τ

ζ

ϰ

ν¹

σ

ϱ

ν²

ξ

ι

θ

η

+30°

HERCULES

ε

R

β

γ

α

δ

Gemma

T

+20°

SERPENS CAPUT

27

CORVUS The Crow

Corvus is a small constellation of the southern hemisphere of the sky. In Greek legends, Corvus is linked with Crater and Hydra. The crow (Corvus) is sent on an errand to fetch water in a cup (Crater), but returns with the water snake (Hydra) instead.

Double star
δ (delta) Corvi is an unequal double for small telescopes, consisting of a 3rd-mag. white star accompanied by a wide 8th-mag. companion.

CRATER The Cup

Crater is an insignificant constellation representing the goblet of Apollo. Its brightest stars are of 4th mag., and there are no objects of interest for amateur observers.

CORVUS / CRATER

28 / 29

CRUX The Southern Cross

The smallest constellation in the sky, Crux is one of the most famous and distinctive. It lies in a rich region of the Milky Way, on the borders of Centaurus.

Bright stars

α (alpha) Crucis (Acrux) is of mag. 0.9 to the naked eye, and is the 14th-brightest star in the sky. But small telescopes split it into two sparkling blue-white components of mags. 1.4 and 1.9.

β (beta) Crucis (Mimosa) is a blue-white star of mag. 1.3.

Double star

μ (mu) Crucis is an easy pair of blue-white stars of 4th and 5th mags. for small telescopes.

Star cluster

NGC 4755 is a showpiece cluster known as the Jewel Box because of its glittering appearance in telescopes. Its brightest star is the 6th-mag. blue supergiant κ (kappa) Crucis; the whole cluster is sometimes termed the κ (kappa) Crucis cluster.

Nebula

The Coalsack is a dark cloud of dust that blots out the bright star background of the Milky Way. The whole of the Coalsack measures 7° x 5°, and extends into neighboring Centaurus and Musca.

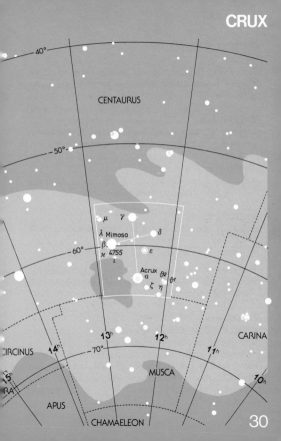

CYGNUS The Swan

A prominent constellation of the northern skies, Cygnus is sometimes known as the Northern Cross because of its cruciform shape. Cygnus represents a swan flying along the Milky Way. In one legend Cygnus is the Greek god Zeus in disguise; another identifies the swan with Orpheus. The Milky Way is particularly rich in the region of Cygnus.

Bright star

α (alpha) Cygni (Deneb, from the Arabic, meaning tail) is a blue-white supergiant star of mag. 1.3.

Variable stars

χ (chi) Cygni is a red giant long-period variable which reaches its brightest, 4th or 5th mag., every 407 days. At its faintest it sinks to 12th mag.

P Cygni is a blue supergiant of 5th mag. which has flared up to 3rd mag. in the past, apparently as a result of throwing off shells of gas.

Double stars

β (beta) Cygni (Albireo) is a beautiful colored double star, one of the showpieces of the sky. It consists of a yellow giant of 3rd mag. accompanied by a 5th-mag. blue-green star visible in small telescopes or even good binoculars. Not to be missed by any observer.

continued

CYGNUS

HERCULES HER

DRACO

LYRA

Vega

HERCULES

CASSIOPEIA

CEPHEUS

Albireo

β

φ

χ

η

κ
ι
θ
6826
ψ
δ

33
26
o²
o¹

ω²
ω¹
α
Deneb

γ
Sadr

ρ

M29

39
41

λ
τ
Gienah
ε
52
6960

6992

VULPECULA

ν

7000
ξ

σ
τ
61

ν

ζ

μ

π¹
π²
M39
W ρ
75

LACERTA

PEGASUS

ANDROMEDA

31

o^1 (omicron^1) Cygni is a 4th-mag. orange giant that forms an attractive wide binocular duo with the 5th-mag. blue giant 30 Cygni. Closer to o^1 (omicron^1) Cygni is a 7th-mag. blue companion visible in binoculars or small telescopes. o^1 (omicron^1) Cygni is an eclipsing binary with a very long period of nearly 10.5 years, which varies by only a few tenths of a mag.

61 Cygni is a famous pair of orange dwarf stars of 5th and 6th mags., easily split in small telescopes. They lie 11.1 l.y. away, and are among the closest neighbors to the Sun.

Planetary nebula
NGC 6828 is known as the Blinking Planetary Nebula, because it seems to blink on and off as one looks alternately at it and away from it. Telescopes of 75mm aperture show its 8th-mag. pale blue disk. The nebula lies within 1° of the 6th-mag. 16 Cygni, an easy double star for small telescopes.

Nebulae
NGC 6992 is the brightest part of the loop that makes up the Veil Nebula; it can only be seen in wide-angle telescopes with low power, or under the very best conditions with binoculars. The Veil Nebula itself is the remains of a supernova that exploded over

continued

50,000 years ago, and consists of a number of faint streamers in a loop-shape – most of it is only seen well on long-exposure photographs.

The Cygnus Rift, also known as the Northern Coalsack, is a dark lane of dust that divides the bright Milky Way in this region, as can be seen by the naked eye on clear nights.

NGC 7000 is a large patch of bright nebulosity known as the North America Nebula because of its shape. Despite its size, it is a difficult object to observe for amateur observers, because of its low surface brightness, but it can be seen in binoculars on clear dark nights.

Black hole
Although by definition invisible, the object known as Cygnus X-1 is thought to be the first black hole ever identified. Its existence is known because it is an X-ray source. It lies near to the star η (eta) Cygni.

Radio galaxy
Cygnus A, near γ (gamma) Cygni, is one of the strongest radio sources known to astronomers. It is a radio galaxy of 18th mag., far beyond the reach of all but large professional telescopes. Long-exposure photographs show Cygnus A as a pair of fuzzy blobs in contact; this is either a galaxy undergoing an explosion or two galaxies in collision.

DELPHINUS The Dolphin

A small constellation in the equatorial region of the sky with a distinctive kite-shape, Delphinus represents a dolphin, one of the messengers of the sea-god Poseidon. Although not bright, its four main stars form a box-shaped group known as Job's Coffin. The peculiar names of two of these stars, Sualocin and Rotanev, first appeared in a star catalog published at Palermo Observatory, Italy, in 1814. Read backwards, they give Nicolaus Venator, which is the Latinized form of Niccolo Cacciatore, the observatory's assistant director at that time. Delphinus lies on the edge of the Milky Way in an area noted for novae.

Double stars

γ (gamma) Delphini is a noted double star consisting of golden and yellow-white stars of 4th and 5th mag., divisible in small telescopes. Struve 2725, a fainter and closer double of 7th and 8th mags., lies nearby in the same field of view.

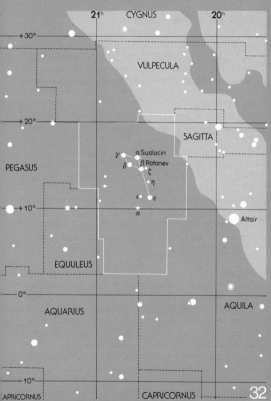

DELPHINUS

CYGNUS

21ʰ

20ʰ

+30°

VULPECULA

+20°

SAGITTA

γ
α Sualocin
δ
β Rotanev
ζ
η

PEGASUS

ι
ε

κ

Altair

+10°

EQUULEUS

0°

AQUARIUS

AQUILA

−10°

APRICORNUS

CAPRICORNUS

32

DORADO The goldfish

A constellation of the southern sky, sometimes also known as the Swordfish, Dorado's main feature is the Large Magellanic Cloud, the larger and more distant of the two satellite galaxies that accompany our Milky Way.

Variable star
β (beta) Doradus is one of the brightest Cepheids, varying from mags. 3.8 to 4.7 every 9 days 20 hours.

Galaxy
The Large Magellanic Cloud is an irregularly-shaped galaxy about 180,000 l.y. away, containing perhaps 10,000 million stars (less than ten per cent of the number in our own Galaxy). It is visible to the naked eye as a hazy patch 6° across, like a detached portion of the Milky Way. Binoculars and small telescopes show that it is richly studded with bright stars, clusters, and nebulae.

Nebula
NGC 2070 is a glowing cloud of hydrogen gas in the Large Magellanic Cloud. It is popularly known as the Tarantula Nebula because of its spidery shape, and is visible to the naked eye as a fuzzy star. At the center of the Tarantula is a cluster of supergiant stars, which includes some of the most massive stars known. Were it as close as the Orion Nebula, it would fill the entire constellation of Orion and cast shadows.

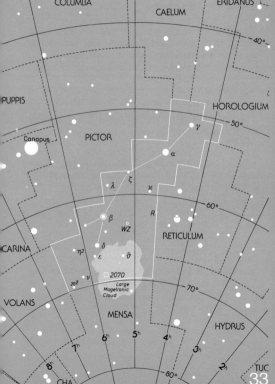

DORADO

COLUMBA

CAELUM

ERIDANUS

CymbalHOROLOGIUM

PUPPIS

PICTOR

Canopus

γ

α

λ ζ
κ

-40°

-50°

-60°

R

RETICULUM

CARINA

β

WZ

δ
η²
ε   ϑ

π²
ν

2070

Large
Magellanic
Cloud

VOLANS

MENSA

HYDRUS

-70°

8ʰ   7ʰ   6ʰ   5ʰ   4ʰ   3ʰ   2ʰ

-80°

CHA

TUC

33

DRACO The Dragon

An extensive constellation of the northern polar region, Draco represents a dragon lying with one of the feet of Hercules firmly planted upon its head.

Double and multiple stars

ν (nu) Draconis is an outstanding binocular pair of 5th-mag. white stars.

ο (omicron) Draconis is a 5th-mag. yellow giant with an 8th-mag. blue companion visible in small telescopes.

ψ (psi) Draconis is a pair of 5th and 6th-mag. yellow stars divisible in small telecopes or even binoculars.

16-17 Draconis is a binocular pair of 5th-mag. blue-white stars. Telescopes show a 7th-mag. companion closer to one of the stars, making a striking triple system.

39 Draconis is another impressive triple system. Binoculars show it as a wide pair of yellow and blue 5th and 7th-mag. stars, but telescopes reveal an 8th-mag. companion closer to the brighter star.

40-41 Draconis is an easy pair of 6th-mag. yellow stars for small telescopes.

continued

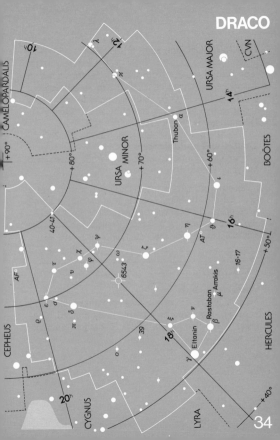

EQUULEUS The Little Horse

The second-smallest constellation, Equuleus lies in the equatorial region of the sky. It is sometimes also called the Foal or Colt, and one legend identifies it as Celeris, the brother of neighboring Pegasus. Its brightest star is of 4th mag.

Double and multiple stars

γ (gamma) Equulei is a 5th-mag. white star with a 6th-mag. binocular companion.

ε (epsilon) Equulei is a 5th-mag. yellow star with a blue-white 7th-mag. companion visible in small telescopes. The brighter (yellow) star is itself double, requiring apertures of 150mm to split it into two close 6th-mag. stars; these orbit each other every 101 years.

Draco continued

Planetary nebula

NGC 6543 is one of the most prominent planetary nebulae, appearing as an irregularly shaped blue-green disk (like an out-of-focus star) in amateur telescopes.

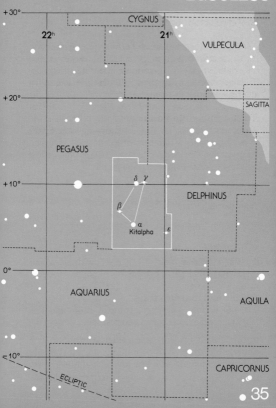

EQUULEUS

CYGNUS

22ʰ

21ʰ

VULPECULA

+30°

+20°

SAGITTA

PEGASUS

+10°

δ γ

β

α
Kitalpha

ε

DELPHINUS

0°

AQUARIUS

AQUILA

−10°

ECLIPTIC

CAPRICORNUS

35

ERIDANUS The River

An extensive constellation, 6th-largest in the sky, Eridanus meanders from the celestial equator far into the southern celestial hemisphere. In Greek legends, Eridanus represents the river into which Phaethon fell after his attempt to drive the chariot of his father the Sun God, but it has also been identified with real rivers such as the Po of Italy, the Nile, and the Euphrates. Despite its size, Eridanus has few bright stars. It contains a number of distant galaxies which are too faint for amateur telescopes, but which show up well on long- exposure photographs.

Bright star

α (alpha) Eridani (Achernar, from the Arabic meaning end of the river) is a blue-white star of mag. 0.5, the 9th-brightest star in the entire sky.

Nearby star

ε (epsilon) Eridani, mag. 3.7, is a yellow dwarf similar to the Sun, lying 10.7 l.y. away.

Double and multiple stars

θ (theta) Eridani is an impressive pair of 3rd and 4th-mag. blue-white stars for small telescopes.

o^2 (omicron^2) Eridani (also called 40 Eridani) is a remarkable triple star containing the most easily observable white dwarf in the sky. The 4th-mag. main

continued

ERIDANUS

ORION

TAURUS

0°

μ ν ξ
β ω
ursa ψ
λ
el

o¹
o²

32

Mira

CETUS

δ ε
π

ζ θ3 θ2
η

10°

S

53

1535

γ

πCet

EPUS

54

τ

20°

τ⁵ τ⁴
τ⁶
τ⁹ τ⁷
τ⁸
τ⁰

τ³ τ²

v¹
v²

30°

v⁴
v³

θ
ι

FORNAX

OLUMBA

CAELUM

θ
ι

Acamar θ ι
s

SCL

40°

e

PHOENIX

HOROLOGIUM

κ

PICTOR

φ χ

Achernar
α

50°

6ʰ 5ʰ 4ʰ 3ʰ 2ʰ HYI 60°

DORADO RETICULUM

36

FORNAX The Furnace

A barren constellation of the southern hemisphere of the sky, originally known as Fornax Chemica (the chemical furnace), Fornax contains a number of faint galaxies, beyond the reach of all but large amateur telescopes, which are its main interest.

Double star

α (alpha) Fornacis is a 4th-mag. yellow star with a close 6th-magcompanion, possibly variable, visible through moderate-sizedamateur telescopes.

Eridanus continued

star is a Sun-like yellow dwarf. Small telescopes show a 10th-mag. companion; this is the white dwarf. Telescopes of 100mm aperture reveal an 11th mag. third member of the system. This is a red dwarf, completing a rare trio that is not to be missed.

32 Eridani, 220 l.y. away, is a beautiful colored double for small telescopes, consisting of 5th and 6th-mag. stars of yellow and blue-green.

Planetary nebula

NGC 1535 is a 9th-mag. planetary nebula visible as a blueish disk in small telescopes.

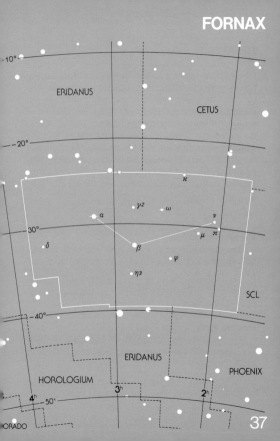

FORNAX

ERIDANUS

CETUS

−10°

−20°

ϰ

γ² ω

α ν

30° μ π

δ β

φ

η³

SCL

−40°

ERIDANUS

PHOENIX

HOROLOGIUM

3ʰ

2ʰ

4ʰ

−50°

ORADO

37

GEMINI The Twins

Gemini is a major zodiacal figure, the Sun passing through the constellation from late June to late July.

Bright stars

α (alpha) Geminorum (Castor) appears of mag. 1.6 to the naked eye. Telescopes of at least 60mm aperture and high magnification split Castor into two blue-white stars of 2nd and 3rd mag. Also visible is a wider 9th-mag. red dwarf. These three stars are spectroscopic binaries, so Castor actually consists of six stars.

β (beta) Geminorum (Pollux) is an orange giant, mag. 1.1.

Variable stars

ζ (zeta) Geminorum is a 4th-mag. Cepheid variable that fluctuates by about 0.4 mag. every 10.2 days.

η (eta) Geminorum is a red giant semi-regular variable. It fluctuates from 3rd to 4th mag. about every 230 days.

Double stars

ε (epsilon) Geminorum is a 3rd-mag. yellow supergiant with a wide 9th-mag. companion visible in small telescopes.

38 Geminorum is an attractive white and yellow pair of 5th and 8th-mag. stars, for small telescopes.

continued

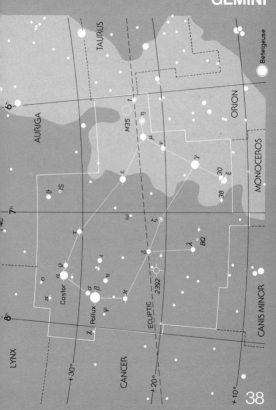

GEMINI

TAURUS

ORION

Betelgeuse

AURIGA

MONOCEROS

LYNX

CANCER

CANIS MINOR

6ʰ

7ʰ

8ʰ

M35

η

μ

ν

γ

ε

ϑ

IS

30

ξ

38

ω

ζ

τ

δ

λ

BQ

ϱ

ι

ν

Castor

α

σ

β

κ

2392

π

o

χ

Pollux

φ

ECLIPTIC

+ 30°

+ 20°

+ 10°

38

GRUS The Crane

A constellation of the southern hemisphere of the sky, Grus represents a water bird, the crane.

Double stars

δ (delta) Gruis is a naked-eye double of 4th-mag. stars.

μ (mu) Gruis is a naked-eye double of 5th-mag. stars.

Gemini continued

Star cluster

M 35 (NGC 2168) is an outstanding cluster of over 100 stars, visible as a misty patch in binoculars; telescopes resolve it into curving chains of stars.

Planetary nebula

NGC 2392 is shown by small telescopes as an 8th-mag. blue-green disk about the size of Jupiter. It is popularly known as the Eskimo or Clown Face Nebula because of its appearance through large telescopes.

Meteors

The Geminid meteors, one of the year's most prominent showers, radiate from near Castor around December 13–14 each year. As many as 60 meteors per hour can be seen, many of them bright and explosive.

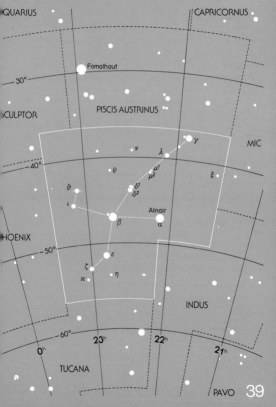

GRUS

AQUARIUS

CAPRICORNUS

Fomalhaut

−30°

PISCIS AUSTRINUS

SCULPTOR

MIC

ν λ γ

−40°

ϱ ω ξ
μ²

ϑ δ¹
ι δ²

β Alnair
α

PHOENIX

−50°

ε

ζ η
κ

INDUS

−60°

0ʰ 23ʰ 22ʰ 21ʰ

TUCANA

PAVO

39

HERCULES

Hercules is a northern hemisphere constellation, and the 5th-largest in the sky. In Greek legends, Hercules was the zon of Zeus, who was given 12 labors in punishment for killing his wife and children in a fit of madness. A group of four stars makes up a shape known as the Keystone, which marks the pelvis of Hercules; on one side of the Keystone lies the celebrated globular cluster M 13, one of the finest objects of its kind.

Variable star

α (alpha) Herculis (Ras Algethi, from the Arabic meaning the kneeler's head) is a red supergiant that varies erratically between 3rd and 4th mag. Small telescopes show that it is also a double star, with a 5th-mag. blue-green companion.

Double stars

ρ (rho) Herculis is a pair of 4th and 5th-mag. blue white stars divisible in small telescopes.

κ (kappa) Herculis is a 5th-mag. yellow giant with a 6th-mag. companion, easily seen in small telescopes.

95 Herculis is an attractive pair of 5th-mag. stars for small telescopes, appearing gold and silver.

continued

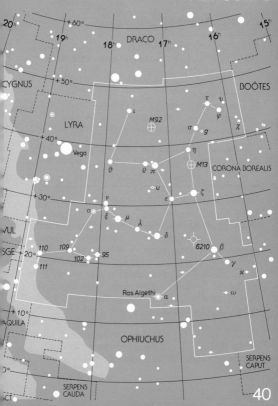

20ʰ · 19ʰ · 18ʰ · 17ʰ · 16ʰ · 15ʰ

+60°

DRACO

CYGNUS

+50°

BOÖTES

τ υ
φ
LYRA

Vega

ι
M92 ⊕
σ g
η

CORONA BOREALIS
M13 ⊕

+40°

ϑ ρ π
ο u

ν
o
ξ
μ λ
δ

ε ζ

+30°

VUL

110 109
102 95

δ

6210 β

SGE

111

γ
κ
ω

Ras Algethi ⊕ α

+10°

AQUILA

OPHIUCHUS

SERPENS
CAPUT

SERPENS
CAUDA

SCT

HOROLOGIUM The Pendulum Clock

A faint and barren constellation of the southern skies, Horologium contains scarcely any objects of note. Its brightest star is of 4th mag.

Variable stars

R Horologii is a red giant long-period variable that fluctuates over a wide range, 5th to 14th mag., approximately every 400 days.

TW Horologii is a deep-red semi-regular variable that fluctuatesbetween 5th and 6th mags.

Hercules continued

Globular clusters

M 13 (NGC 6205) contains 300,000 stars, and is the brightest globular cluster in the northern skies, a showpiece for all apertures. It is visible to the naked eye as a 6th-mag. misty patch on clear nights, and is prominent in binoculars. Small telescopes begin to resolve the cluster into stars, giving it the appearance of a mottled mound of sparkling stardust. M 13 lies about 22,500 l.y. away.

M 92 (NGC 6341) is a smaller and somewhat fainter cluster than M 13, but readily visible in binoculars. It is more condensed at the center than M 13.

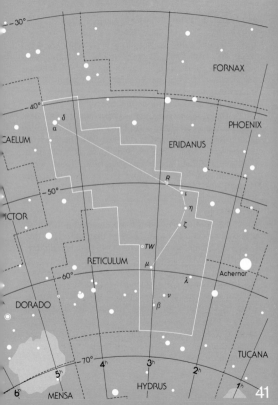

HOROLOGIUM

-30°

FORNAX

-40°

CAELUM

δ
α

ERIDANUS

PHOENIX

-50°

R

ι

η

ζ

PICTOR

TW

RETICULUM

μ

Achernar

-60°

λ

ν

β

DORADO

TUCANA

-70°   4ʰ   3ʰ

5ʰ

6ʰ

MENSA

HYDRUS

2ʰ

1ʰ

41

HYDRA The Water Snake

Hydra is the largest constellation in the sky, yet it is far from prominent. Its most readily recognizable feature is a group of stars that make up its head, lying just north of the celestial equator. From there its tail snakes away to the southwest, toward Centaurus and Lupus; the total length of the constellation is over 100°. In Greek mythology, Hydra was the multi-headed monster slain by Hercules as one of his 12 labors. In another legend it is linked with the story of the crow, Corvus, who was sent to fetch water in a cup, represented by the constellation Crater. The constellations of Corvus and Crater are found on Hydra's back.

Bright star

α (alpha) Hydrae (Alphard, from the Arabic meaning solitary one) is an orange giant of mag. 2.0. It is the only star in the entire constellation that is brighter than mag. 3.0.

Variable stars

R Hydrae is a red giant long-period variable similar to Mira in Cetus. It fluctuates between 4th and 10th mags. every 386 days.

U Hydrae is a deep-red irregular variable star, that fluctuates between 5th and 6th mags. with no set period.

Double stars

ε (epsilon) Hydrae is a challenging double star, consisting of yellow and blue components, of 3rd and 7th mag., that require at least 75mm aperture to be separated.

27 Hydrae is a 5th-mag. yellow giant with a very wide 7th-mag. binocular companion. Small telescopes reveal that this star itself has a 9th-mag. companion.

54 Hydrae is a 5th-mag. yellow giant with a 7th-mag. purple companion for small telescopes.

1 Hydrae is a 5th-mag. blue-white star with a wide 8th-mag. companion visible in small telescopes or good binoculars.

Star cluster

M 48 (NGC 2548) is a large binocular cluster of about 80 stars of 9th mag. and fainter, arranged in a triangular shape. Small telescopes resolve the brightest of its individual stars.

Planetary nebula

NGC 3242 is a 9th-mag. planetary nebula for small telescopes. It appears as a hazy blue-green disk known as the Ghost of Jupiter because of its similarity to the telescopic appearance of that planet.

continued on p. 128

HYDRUS The Lesser Water Snake

Hydrus is an insignificant constellation of the south polar region of the sky. Its brightest stars are of 3rd mag.

Double star

π (pi) Hydra is a wide binocular or naked-eye pair of unrelated 5th-mag. red and orange stars.

Hydra continued

Globular cluster

M 68 (NGC 4590) is a small, 8th-mag. globular cluster, unspectacular in small instruments; apertures of 150mm are needed to resolve its individual stars.

Galaxy

M 83 (NGC 5236) is an impressive 8th-mag. spiral galaxy seen face-on, and is one of the brightest of its kind in the southern sky. Through small telescopes it appears as a misty patch with a bright nucleus; apertures of 150mm are needed to trace its spiral arms.

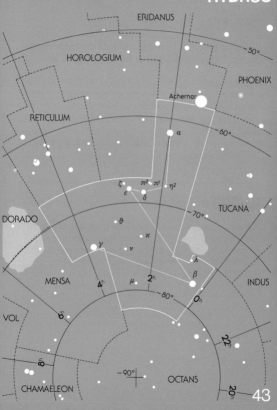

HYDRUS

ERIDANUS

HOROLOGIUM

PHOENIX

−50°

RETICULUM

Achernar

α

−60°

ζ
π² π¹ η²
ε δ

TUCANA

ϑ

−70°

DORADO

κ

γ

ν

λ

MENSA

μ

β

INDUS

4ʰ

2ʰ

0ʰ

−80°

VOL

δ

22ʰ

CHAMAELEON

−90°

OCTANS

20ʰ

43

INDUS The Indian

A faint constellation of the southern hemisphere of the sky, Indus represents a native American Indian.

Nearby star
ε (epsilon) Indi is a yellow dwarf star similar to the Sun, 11.2 l.y. away, appearing of mag. 4.7.

Double star
θ (theta) Indi is a pair of 5th and 7th-mag. stars that can be separated by small telescopes.

LACERTA The Lizard

A very inconspicuous constellation of the northern hemisphere of the sky, Lacerta is sandwiched between Andromeda and Cygnus. Its brightest stars are of 4th mag. Lacerta lies in the Milky Way and has been the site of three bright novae this century, but it contains no objects of note for users of small telescopes.

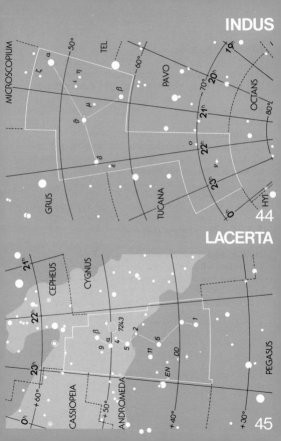

INDUS

MICROSCOPIUM

TEL

PAVO

OCTANS

α
ξ
ι
η
β
μ
ϑ
δ
ε

50°
60°
70°
80°

19ʰ
20ʰ
21ʰ
22ʰ
23ʰ
0ʰ

GRUS

TUCANA

HYI

o
ν

44

LACERTA

CEPHEUS

CYGNUS

CASSIOPEIA

ANDROMEDA

PEGASUS

21ʰ
22ʰ
23ʰ
0ʰ

+60°
+50°
+40°
+30°

β
α
724.3
2
9
4
5
11
6
1
EN
DD

45

LEO The Lion

Leo is a constellation of the zodiac, through which the Sun passes from mid-August to mid-September. It represents the lion slain by Hercules as part of his 12 labors.

Bright star

α (alpha) Leonis (Regulus, the little king) is a blue-white star of mag. 1.4. Binoculars and small telescopes show a wide 8th-mag. companion.

Variable star

R Leonis is a red giant long-period variable that fluctuates between 5th and 10th mags. with an average period of about 310 days.

Double and multiple stars

γ (gamma) Leonis (Algieba, Lion's mane) is a showpiece pair of yellow giants of 2nd and 3rd mags. divisible in small telescopes. In binoculars as unrelated 5th-mag. star, 40 Leonis is seen nearby.

ζ (zeta) Leonis is an optical triple star of 3rd mag. In binoculars ζ (zeta) Leonis appears to have two companions of 6th mag. at different distances from it, but both are unrelated to it.

τ (tau) Leonis is a 5th-mag. orange giant with a 7th-mag. binocular companion.

continued

LEO MINOR The Lesser Lion

A faint and obscure constellation of northern skies, sandwiched between Ursa Major and Leo, Leo Minor contains no objects for users of small instruments.

Leo continued

Galaxies

Leo contains a number of interesting galaxies, none particularly easy for small telescopes. M 65 (NGC 3623) and M 66 (NGC 3627) are a pair of spiral galaxies of 9th and 8th mag. repssectively; M 66 is presented at an angle to us and appears cigar-shaped. M 95 (NGC 3351) and M 96 (NGC 3368) are two more spiral galaxies, of 10th and 9th mags. All these objects require low power and a dark night to be picked out as faint smudges.

Meteors

The yearly Leonid meteor shower appears around November 17, radiating from a point near γ (gamma) Leonis. Usually the numbers are low, peaking at about 10 per hour, but occasionally tremendous storms of up to 100,000 meteors per hour have been seen. These storms occur when the Earth passes near to the parent comet, Tempel-Tuttle, which has an orbital period of 33 years. The last such storm was in 1966; another spectacular Leonid meteor storm may occur in 1999.

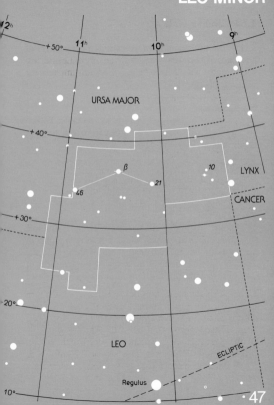

LEO MINOR

12ʰ

+50°

11ʰ

10ʰ

9ʰ

URSA MAJOR

β

21

10

LYNX

46

CANCER

+40°

+30°

+20°

LEO

+10°

Regulus

ECLIPTIC

47

LEPUS The Hare

Lepus is a constellation of the southern hemisphere of the sky. Although overshadowed by neighboring Orion and Canis Major, it is not without interest for amateur observers.

Variable star

R Leporis is a deep-red long-period variable, known as Hind's Crimson Star. It varies from 6th to 10th mags. about every 430 days.

Double star

γ (gamma) Leporis is an attractive binocular duo of yellow and orange stars, of 4th and 6th matgs.

Star cluster

NGC 2017 is a star cluster that is really a multiple star. Binoculars and small telescopes show a group of five stars of 6th to 10th mag. Two of these stars are themselves close doubles, as revealed by apertures of 150mm, making this a group of at least seven related stars.

Globular cluster

M 79 (NGC 1904) is a compact 8th-mag. globular cluster for small telescopes. It lies near a 5th-mag. triple star, Herschel 3752, also visible in small telescopes.

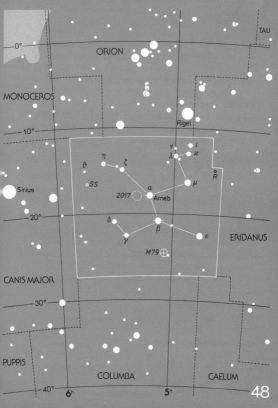

LEPUS

TAU

0°

ORION

MONOCEROS

Rigel

−10°

η
θ   ζ
SS
2017   α
Arneb

ν   ι
λ   κ
μ
R

Sirius

−20°   ERIDANUS

δ   β
γ   ε

M79

CANIS MAJOR

−30°

PUPPIS

COLUMBA   CAELUM

6ʰ   5ʰ   48

LIBRA The Scales

A faint constellation of the zodiac through which the Sun passes during November, Libra is now seen as the scales of Astraea, goddess of justice, but once represented the claws of neighboring Scorpius.

Variable star

δ (delta) Librae is an eclipsing binary of the same type as Algol. It varies between mags. 4.8 and 5.9 every 2 days 8 hours.

Double and multiple stars

α (alpha) Librae (Zubenelgenubi, from the Arabic meaning southern claw) is a 3rd-mag. blue-white star with a wide 5th-mag. companion easily visible in binoculars.

ι (iota) Librae is a complex multiple star. To the naked eye it appears of 4th mag. Binoculars show a wide 6th-mag. companion, 25 Librae. In small telescopes another, fainter companion is visible; apertures of 75mm show that this companion actually consists of a close pair of 10th-mag. stars.

μ (mu) Librae is a 6th-mag. star with a close 7th-mag. companion for telescopes of 75mm aperture.

Globular cluster

NGC 5897 is a 10th-mag. globular cluster with loosely scattered stars, unspectacular in small instruments.

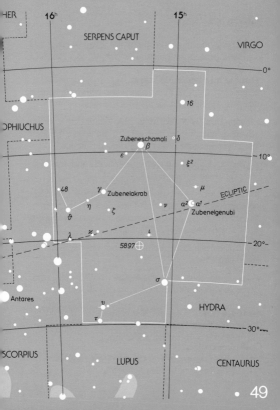

LIBRA

HER

16ʰ

SERPENS CAPUT

15ʰ

VIRGO

0°

OPHIUCHUS

16

Zubeneschamali
β

δ

ε

10°

ξ²

48

γ Zubenelakrab

μ

ECLIPTIC

η

ζ

ν

α² α¹

Zubenelgenubi

θ

λ

κ

ι

5897 ⊕

20°

σ

Antares

υ

HYDRA

τ

30°

SCORPIUS

LUPUS

CENTAURUS

49

LUPUS The Wolf

A constellation of the southern sky, Lupus is depicted as a wolf held in the grasp of neighboring Centaurus.

Double and multiple stars

ε (epsilon) Lupi is a 3rd-mag. blue-white star with a 9th-mag. companion for small telescopes.

η (eta) Lupi is a 3rd-mag. blue-white star with an 8th-mag. companion, not easy to see in the smallest telescopes because of the brightness difference.

κ (kappa) Lupi is an easy pair of 4th and 6th-mag. stars for small telescopes.

μ (mu) Lupi is a 4th-mag. star with a 7th-mag. companion visible in small telescopes. Telescopes of at least 100mm aperture show that this companion is itself a tight pair of 5th-mag. stars.

ζ (xi) Lupi is a neat pair of 5th and 6th-mag. stars for small telescopes.

π (pi) Lupi consists of a close pair of 5th-mag. stars, divisible with apertures of 75mm and above.

Star cluster

NGC 5822 is a large cluster of at least 100 faint stars for binoculars and small telescopes.

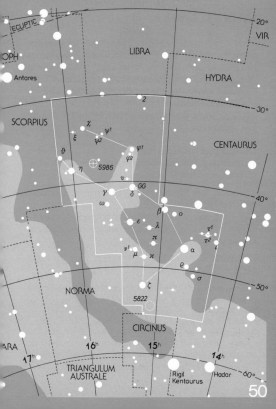

LUPUS

ECLIPTIC

20°

VIR

OPH

LIBRA

Antares

HYDRA

30°

SCORPIUS

CENTAURUS

χ

ξ

ψ¹

ψ²

φ¹

θ

η

⊕ 5986

φ²

ν

GG

40°

γ

δ

ω

β

ο

ε

λ

τ¹

τ²

π

ι

ν¹

α

μ

κ

ϱ

σ

ζ

50°

NORMA

5822

CIRCINUS

ARA

17ʰ

16ʰ

15ʰ

14ʰ

60°

TRIANGULUM
AUSTRALE

Rigil
Kentaurus

Hadar

50

LYNX The Lynx

Lynx is an exceedingly faint constellation of northern skies named by the Polish astronomer Johannes Hevelius because only the "lynx-eyed" would be able to see it. Changes of constellation boundaries have produced confusion in the stellar nomenclature of this region. For instance, Lynx contains the star 10 Ursae Majoris, while the star known as 41 Lyncis lies in Ursa Major.

Double and multiple stars

5 Lyncis is a 5th-mag. orange giant with an 8th-mag. companion visible in small telescopes.

12 Lyncis is a 5th-mag. blue-white star with an 8th-mag. companion for small telescopes. In apertures of 75mm or more, the brighter component is seen to have a much closer 6th-mag. companion, making 12 Lyncis a triple star.

19 Lyncis is a neat pair of 6th-mag. stars for small telescopes.

38 Lyncis is a tight pair of 4th and 6th mag. stars that provide a challenge for small telescopes because of their closeness.

41 Lyncis is to be found over the border in Ursa Major (page 222). Small telescopes show it to be an interesting triple star, consisting of components of 5th, 8th and 10th mags., arranged in a triangle.

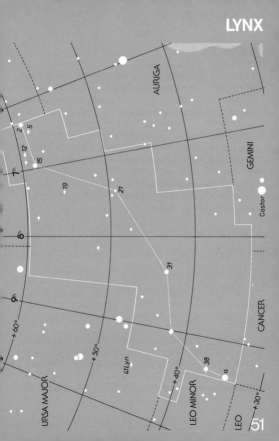

LYNX

AURIGA

GEMINI

Castor

2
5
12
15
7ʰ
19
21
8ʰ
31
9ʰ
38
α

+60°
+50°
+40°
+30°

URSA MAJOR

41 Lyn

LEO MINOR

CANCER

LEO

51

LYRA The Lyre

A prominent constellation of the northern hemisphere of the sky, Lyra represents the harp of Orpheus; the neighboring constellation of Cygnus is sometimes visualized as Orpheus himself.

Bright star

α (alpha) Lyrae (Vega, from the Arabic meaning stone eagle) is a brilliant blue-white star of mag. 0.0, the fifth-brightest star in the entire sky. It lies 26 l.y. away. Vega forms one corner of the Summer Triangle of three bright stars, completed by Deneb in Cygnus and Altair in Aquila.

Variable and double stars

β (beta) Lyrae is an eclipsing cream-colored binary star that varies from mags. 3.4 to 4.3 every 12 days 22 hours. (For a comparison chart, see page 147.) Small telescopes resolve β (beta) Lyrae as an attractive double star, with a blue companion of 8th mag. (In addition there are two wider 9th-mag. companions that can be seen in small telescopes.)

δ (delta) Lyrae is another double variable. Binoculars show one blue-white star, mag. 6.0, and a red giant semi-regular variable, which varies erratically between 4th and 5th mags.

continued

ε (epsilon) Lyrae is the most celebrated quadruple star in the sky, commonly known as the Double Double. Binoculars, or even keen eyesight, show it to consist of a wide pair of 5th-mag. white stars. But each star is itself a close double, requiring at least 60mm or 75mm aperture and high magnification to be split.

ζ (zeta) Lyrae is an easy double star of 4th and 6th mags. for binoculars or small telescopes.

Planetary nebula
M 57 (NGC 6720) is the famous Ring Nebula, beautifully shown on long-exposure photographs (see opposite) but somewhat disappointing in amateur telescopes. It is easy to find, midway between β (beta) and γ (gamma) Lyrae. Small telescopes show it as a ghostly elliptical disk on dark nights, larger than the apparent size of Jupiter. Its brightness is similar to that of a 9th-mag. star out of focus. Apertures of at least 150mm are needed to show its central hole, but its faint central star is beyond the reach of amateur telescopes.

Meteors
Two meteor showers radiate from Lyra each year, neither of them particularly plentiful. The stronger and brighter shower, the April Lyrids, peak at about 15 meteors per hour on April 21–22. The June Lyrids reach about 8 per hour on June 16.

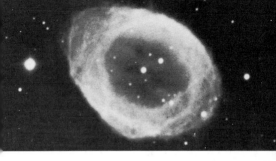

The Ring Nebula in Lyra, M 57, is a famous example of a planetary nebula. *Hale Observatories*

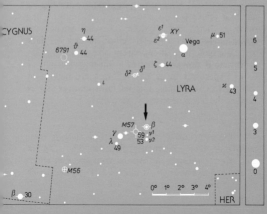

MENSA The Table Mountain

A faint and obscure constellation of the south polar region of the sky, Mensa's main point of interest is that part of the Large Magellanic Cloud strays over the border into it from Dorado. The brightest stars of Mensa are of 5th mag., and there are no objects of note for owners of small telescopes.

MICROSCOPIUM The Microscope

A faint constellation of the southern hemisphere of the sky, Microscopium's brightest stars are of 5th mag., and it contains scarcely any objects of interest for owners of small telescopes.

Double star
α (alpha) Microscopii is a 5th-mag. yellow giant with a 10th-mag.companion visible in small telescopes.

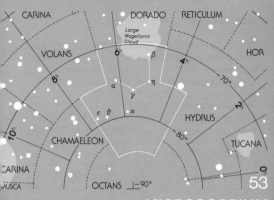

MENSA

CARINA

VOLANS

DORADO   RETICULUM

Large
Magellanic
Cloud

β

6ʰ

η

4ʰ

HOR

8°

α

γ

−70°

ε   ϑ   κ

2ʰ

ε   ϑ

HYDRUS

10°

−80°

CHAMAELEON

TUCANA

CARINA

0ʰ

MUSCA

OCTANS ⊥−90°

53

MICROSCOPIUM

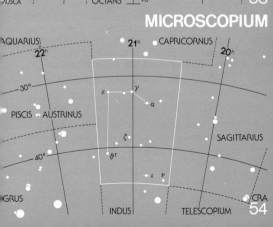

AQUARIUS

21ʰ   CAPRICORNUS

22ʰ

20ʰ

−30°

ε   γ

PISCIS AUSTRINUS

α

ζ

SAGITTARIUS

−40°

ϑ¹

ι   ν

GRUS

INDUS

TELESCOPIUM

CRA

54

MONOCEROS The Unicorn

A constellation of the equatorial region of the sky, Monoceros is overshadowed by the brilliance of neighboring Orion but nevertheless containing several interesting clusters and nebulae.

Variable star

S Monocerotis is an erratically variable supergiant which fluctuates between 4th and 5th mags. with no set period. It has an 8th-mag. companion, difficult to see in the smallest telescopes because of its closeness. S Monocerotis is the brightest member of the star cluster NGC 2264 (see page 152).

Double and multiple stars

β (beta) Monocerotis is an outstanding triple star for telescopes of all apertures. The three blue-white stars, of 4th, 5th, and 6th mags., are arranged in an arc, the two faintest stars being closest together.

δ (delta) Monocerotis, a blue-white star of 4th mag., has a wide but unrelated 5th-mag. companion, 21 Monocerotis, visible to the naked eye or binoculars.

ε (epsilon) Monocerotis is an attractive double for small telescopes, consisting of yellow and blue stars of 4th and 7th mag.

continued

LEPUS

IC2

Betelgeuse

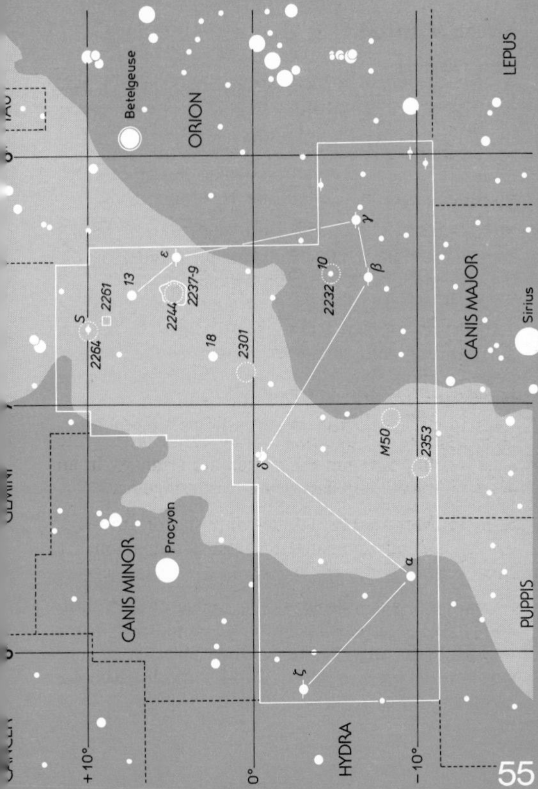

ORION

γ

ε

13

β

10

2232

2261

2237-9

S

2244

18

CANIS MAJOR

2264

2301

Sirius

δ

M50

2353

GEMINI

CANIS MINOR

Procyon

α

PUPPIS

ζ

+10°

0°

HYDRA

−10°

55

Star clusters

M 50 (NGC 2323) is a 6th-mag. binocular cluster. Telescopes resolve over 100 individual stars, including an orange giant at the center.

NGC 2232 is a scattered binocular cluster centered on the 5th-mag. blue-white star 10 Monocerotis.

NGC 2244 is a binocular cluster of about 20 young stars born from a faint surrounding nebulosity, the Rosette Nebula. A 5th-mag. orange giant star, 12 Monocerotis, that appears to be part of the cluster, is actually an unrelated foreground star. The nebula surrounding this cluster is known as the Rosette because of its flower-like shape. Unfortunately, the Rosette Nebula is too faint for amateur telescopes, but its full beauty shows up on long-exposure photographs.

NGC 2264 is another cluster embedded in a nebula. Binoculars show a group of about 20 stars, including the variable S Monocerotis (see previous page) arranged in a triangular shape. Long-exposure photographs show faint surrounding nebulosity. At its southern end is an intruding wedge of dark dust, known as the Cone Nebula due to its tapered shape. NGC 2264 is estimated to lie about 300 l.y. away, a similar distance to NGC 2244 and the Rosette Nebula.

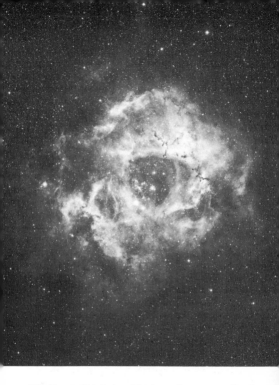

The Rosette Nebula is a faint loop of gas surrounding the star cluster NGC 2244 in Monoceros. *Hale Observatories*

MUSCA The Fly

A small constellation in the south polar region of the sky, Musca was originally known as Apis (the bee). Part of the dark Coalsack Nebula spills over into Musca from neighboring Crux, the Southern Cross.

Double stars

β (beta) Muscae appears to the naked eye as a blue-white star of mag. 3. Telescopes of 100mm aperture show that it actually consists of a close pair of 4th-mag. stars.

θ (theta) Muscae is a 5th-mag. star with a 7th-mag. companion for small telescopes. Its companion is a small, hot star of the type known as a Wolf-Rayet star (a rare class of stars with very hot surfaces which seem to be ejecting gas.)

Musca, shown under its old name of Apis, the Bee, on the 1801 atlas of Johann Bode. *Royal Greenwich Observatory*

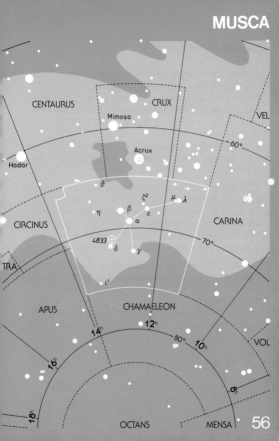

NORMA The Level

A small constellation of the southern hemisphere of the sky, Norma represents a surveyor's level. Its boundaries have been changed since it was first formed, so that it no longer contains the stars that were originally labelled α (alpha) and β (beta).

Double stars

γ^1 γ^2 (gamma^1 gamma^2) Normae are an unrelated pair of yellow stars of 4th and 5th mags.

ε (epsilon) Normae is a 5th-mag. star with an 8th-mag. companion visible in small telescopes. Professional observations have found that both stars are spectroscopic binaries, (spectroscopic binaries are two stars that are too close together to be divided through a telescope) making a four-star system.

ι^1 (iota^1) Normae is a 5th-mag. star with an 8th-mag. companion for small telescopes.

Star cluster

NGC 6087 is a large binocular cluster of about 35 stars including the 6th-mag. Cepheid variable S Normae.

NORMA

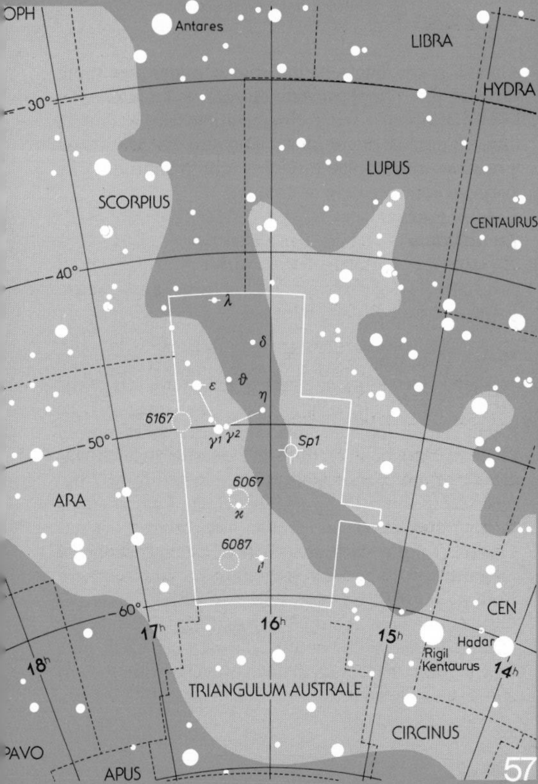
OPH
Antares
LIBRA
HYDRA
-30°
LUPUS
SCORPIUS
CENTAURUS
-40°
λ
δ
ε
ϑ
η
6167
γ1 γ2
-50°
Sp1
6067
ϰ
ARA
6087
ι1
-60°
CEN
17h
16h
15h
Hadar
Rigil
Kentaurus
14h
18h
TRIANGULUM AUSTRALE
CIRCINUS
PAVO
APUS

OCTANS The Octant

Octans is the constellation that contains the south celestial pole. Appropriately enough, it represents an old instrument used for navigation, the octant, a forerunner of the sextant. Despite its privileged position, the constellation is not prominent; its brightest stars are only of 4th mag.

Double star

λ (lambda) Octantis is a double star for small telescopes, consisting of yellow and white components of 5th and 8th mag.

South Pole star

σ (sigma) Octantis is the nearest naked-eye star to the south celestial pole. It is a white star of mag. 5.5; its distance from Earth is unknown. Currently σ (sigma) Octantis lies about 1° from the celestial pole. It was closest to the celestial pole in the nineteenth century, when it lay about 45' away. The effect of precession is moving the celestial pole further away from σ (sigma) Octantis into a blank area of sky in the direction of Chamaeleon. The next reasonably bright southern pole star will be the wide double δ (delta) Chamaeleontis in about 2000 years' time. To find the exact position of the south celestial pole itself, note that it forms a near-equilateral triangle with χ (chi) and τ (tau) Octantis.

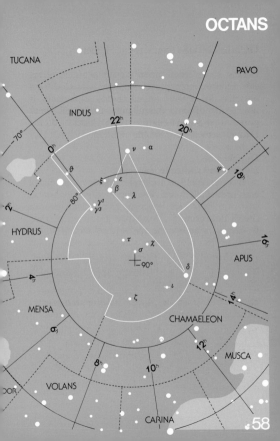

OPHIUCHUS The Serpent Holder

A large constellation of the equatorial region of the sky, Ophiuchus represents a man encoiled by a serpent (the constellation Serpens). Ophiuchus is usually identified as Aesculapius, a mythical Greek healer. The Sun passes through Ophiuchus during December each year, but the constellation is not part of the zodiac.

Double and multiple stars

ρ (rho) Ophiuchi is a complex multiple star. Small telescopes show it as a close pair of 5th and 6th-mag. stars with two wide 8th-mag. companions, one on each side, forming a V-shaped grouping. ρ (rho) Ophiuchi is embedded in faint nebulosity which shows up only on long-exposure photographs.

τ (tau) Ophiuchi is a close pair of 5th and 6th-mag. stars requiring at least 100mm aperture and high magnification to be divided.

36 Ophiuchi is a neat pair of 5th-mag. orange stars for small telescopes.

70 Ophiuchi is a close but beautiful double star consisting of yellow and orange components of 4th and 6th mag. At least 100mm aperture and high magnification is needed to split them. At a distance of 17 l.y., 70 Ophiuchi is relatively near to us.

continued

OPHIUCHUS

Ras Alhague
α

ι
κ

72

6633

66 72

14665
β   σ

6572

66
67

70

SERPENS
CAPUT

λ

68

γ

M14

M12

M10

Yed Prior

δ

Yed Posterion

ε

τ
ν

μ

ζ

ν

M107

SCUTUM

SERPENS CAUDA

φ
χ

η
Sabik

M9

ω
ψ

ξ

ECLIPTIC

ρ

SAGITTARIUS

44
ϑ

o

M19

36

Antares

45

M62

SCORPIUS

Nearby star

Barnard's Star, 6 l.y. away, is the next-closest star to the Sun after the triple system of α (alpha) Centauri. It is a red dwarf of mag. 9.5, within the range of small telescopes. The finder chart opposite will help you locate this elusive but fascinating object. Barnard's Star has the largest proper motion of any star; it moves across 1° of sky every 350 years. Some observations suggest that Barnard's Star is accompanied by one or two large planets similar to Jupiter and Saturn.

Star clusters

IC 4665 is an easy binocular cluster consisting of a loose scattering of about 20 stars of mag. 7 and fainter covering 1° of sky, visible in the same field as the 3rd-mag. yellow giant β (beta) Ophiuchi.

NGC 6633 is a binocular cluster of over 60 stars.

Globular clusters

M 10 (NGC 6254) and M 12 (NGC 6218), of 7th and 8th mag., are the most prominent of several globular clusters visible in Ophiuchus. In binoculars or small telescopes they appear as misty patches. Of the two, M 10 appears the more condensed.

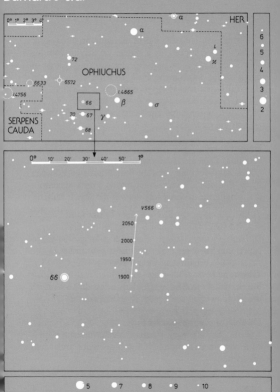

ORION The Hunter

A magnificent constellation of the equatorial region of the sky, Orion represents a hunter or warrior with his shield and club raised against the snorting charge of neighboring Taurus the Bull. In Greek mythology, boastful Orion was stung to death by a scorpion, and is now placed in the sky so that he sets in the west as his slayer, represented by the constellation Scorpius, rises in the east.

Bright stars

α (alpha) Orionis (Betelgeuse) is a red supergiant star and a semi-regular variable that fluctuates between mags. 0.4 and 1.3 with no set period. At its maximum it is among the 10 brightest stars in the sky. It pulsates in diameter between about 300 and 400 times the size of the Sun. It lies 310 l.y. away.

β (beta) Orionis (Rigel, giant's leg) is a blue-white supergiant of mag. 0.1, the 7th-brightest star in the sky and the brightest in Orion. Rigel is about 900 l.y. distant, and has a 7th-mag. companion that is difficult for the smallest telescopes to distinguish because of the overpowering glare from Rigel itself.

Double and multiple stars

δ (delta) Orionis is a 2nd-mag. blue-white star with a wide 7th-mag. companion for binoculars and small telescopes.

continued

164

ζ (zeta) Orionis (Alnitak, the girdle) consists of a tight pair of 2nd and 4th-mag. stars requiring at least 75mm aperture and high magnification to be split. There is also a wider 10th-mag. companion.

η (eta) Orionis is a difficult pair of 4th and 5th-mag. stars for apertures of 100mm and above

θ¹ (theta¹) Orionis, also known as the Trapezium, is a multiple star at the heart of the Orion Nebula. This group of stars has been formed from the gas of the Orion Nebula, and their light makes it glow. Small telescopes show a rectangular arrangement of four stars ranging from 5th to 8th mag. There are also two other 11th-mag. stars in the group, visible with apertures of 100mm.

θ² (theta²) Orionis lies near to θ¹ (theta¹) Orionis, and is a binocular duo of 5th and 6th-mag stars.

ι (iota) Orionis is an unequal double star for small telescopes, of 3rd and 7th mag. Also visible in the same field is a wider double of 5th and 6th mag. known as Struve 747.

λ (lambda) Orionis is a tight pair of 4th and 6th-mag. stars for small telescopes.

σ (sigma) Orionis is a stunning multiple star. Binoculars show that this 4th-mag. blue-white star has a 7th-mag. companion. Small telescopes reveal

continued

Orion Nebulae

□ M78

δ Mintaka

31

ε Alnilam   VV

I.432 □ □ I.431

2024   ζ Alnitak

I.435
Horsehead Nebula   I.434

σ

1981

1973-5-7

45 42

M 43   θ¹

θ²   M 42
The Great
Orion Nebula

ι

0°   20'   40'   1°

two closer companions of 7th and 10th mag., giving σ (sigma) Orionis the appearance of a moon with planets. Also in the same telescopic field is the triple star Struve 761, consisting of a thin triangle of 8th and 9th-mag stars, completing a delightfully rich grouping.

Star cluster

NGC 1981 is a scattered binocular cluster of 10 stars, including the double star Struve 750, a pair of 6th and 8th-mag. stars for small telescopes.

Nebulae

M 42 (NGC 1976) and M 43 (NGC 1982) together form one of the most celebrated objects in the entire heavens: the great Orion Nebula, a cloud of gas and dust fully 1° across in which stars are being born. The Nebula itself is visible to the naked eye as a misty haze making up the sword of Orion. It is prominent in binoculars, and is breathtaking in telescopes under low powers which reveal indescribably complex twists and swirls of gas. Visually, the Orion Nebula seems to be in two parts, M 42 and M 43, but photographs show that these are both part of the same large cloud separated by a dark intrusion known as the Fish Mouth. To the human eye the Orion Nebula appears greenish, as do most nebulae, but photographs show that its true color is reddish-orange. The reason for this color difference is that the human eye has poor sensitivity to colors at such low light levels. At the heart of the Orion Nebula is the multiple star θ^1 (theta^1) Orionis (see above), which lights up the surrounding gas. The Orion Nebula lies 1300 l.y. away and has a diameter of 15 l.y. It is estimated to contain enough gas to make a cluster of thousands of stars.

NGC 1977 is a patch of nebulosity north of the Orion Nebula. It surrounds the 5th-mag. stars 42 and 45 Orionis. Although visible in small telescopes, NGC 1977 is often overlooked in favor of its more impressive neighbor, M 42.

The Horsehead Nebula is a strikingly shaped dark nebula, that looks like the black knight in a celestial chess game. It is caused by a cloud of dark dust that overlays the tenuous nebulosity IC 434 which stretches southward from ζ (zeta) Orionis. However, IC 434 is visually highly elusive in even the largest amateur telescopes and the Horsehead itself is all but invisible, so observers must be content with views of this remarkable object provided by long-exposure photographs.

Meteors
The Orionid meteors reach their peak around October 21 each year, when as many as 20 meteors per hour may be seen coming from a point near the border with Gemini.

PAVO The Peacock

A modest constellation of the southern celestial hemisphere, Pavo represents the bird that was sacred to the goddess of the heavens, Juno.

Bright star
α (alpha) Pavonis (Peacock) is a blue-white star of mag. 1.9.

Variable star
κ (kappa) Pavonis is a pulsating variable of the W Virginis type. It is a yellow supergiant that varies from mag. 3.9 to mag. 4.8 every 9 days 1 hour 36 minutes.

Double star
ζ (xi) Pavonis is an unequal double star consisting of a 4th-mag. red giant with a 9th-mag. companion, made difficult in small telescopes because it becomes lost in the primary's glare.

Globular cluster
NGC 6752 is a large 7th-mag. globular cluster for binoculars and small telescopes. Within its outer regions lies a tight 8th-mag. double star, but this is apparently a foreground object.

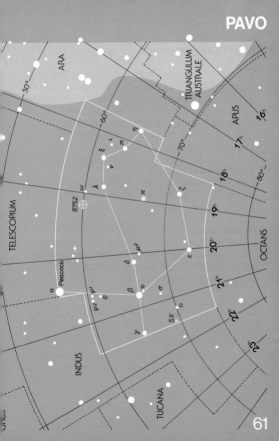

PAVO

ARA

TRIANGULUM
AUSTRALE

APUS

OCTANS

TELESCOPIUM

INDUS

TUCANA

Peacock

6752

61

PEGASUS The Winged Horse

A large constellation in the northern half of the sky, Pegasus represents the winged horse of Greek mythology. A feature of the constellation is the Great Square of Pegasus whose corners are marked out by four stars; one of these stars, originally known as δ (delta) Pegasi, is now assigned to neighboring Andromeda.

Variable star

α (beta) Pegasi (Scheat, shoulder) is a red giant irregular variable that fluctuates between 2nd and 3rd mag. with no set period.

Double stars

ε (epsilon) Pegasi is a double star with components of widely unequal brightness. ε (epsilon) Pegasi itself is a 2nd-mag. yellow supergiant; its companion, visible in small telescopes or even binoculars, is of 9th mag.

1 Pegasi is a 4th-mag. yellow giant with a 9th-mag. companion for small telescopes.

Globular cluster

M 15 (NGC 7078) is one of the finest globular clusters in the northern sky. It is a 6th-mag. object visible in binoculars and small telescopes, which show it as a glorious misty patch in an attractive field. Apertures of 150mm are needed to resolve individual stars.

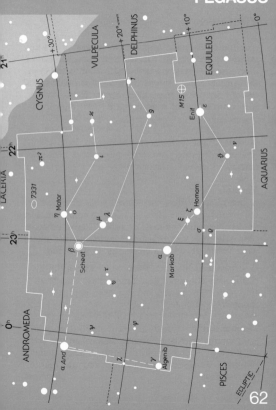

21ʰ
+30°
+20°
+10°
0°

CYGNUS
VULPECULA
DELPHINUS
EQUULEUS

κ
γ
9
Enif
M15 ⊕
ε

22ʰ
π²
ι
ν
ϑ

LACERTA
7331
η Matar
ο
λ
μ
ξ ζ Homam
σ
ϱ
AQUARIUS

23ʰ
β
Scheat
α
Markab

τ
υ

0ʰ
ψ
φ
χ
γ
Algenib

ANDROMEDA
α And

PISCES
ECLIPTIC

PERSEUS

A constellation of the northern sky, Perseus represents the hero of Greek mythology who saved Andromeda from being devoured by the sea monster Cetus. In the sky, Perseus is depicted as holding the severed head of Medusa the Gorgon, whose evil eye is represented by the winking star β (beta) Persei.

Bright star

α (alpha) Persei is a yellow supergiant of mag. 1.8. It lies within a widely scattered cluster that forms an attractive star field in binoculars.

Variable stars

β (beta) Persei (Algol, the demon) is the prototype of the eclipsing binary variables. This type of variable consists of two stars in close orbit that periodically pass in front of each other, as seen from Earth. Algol itself varies from mag. 2.2 to 3.5 every 2 days 21 hours. For a chart, see page 177.

ρ (rho) Persei is a red giant semi-regular variable that fluctuates between 3rd and 4th mag. approximately monthly.

Double stars

ε (epsilon) Persei is a 3rd-mag. blue-white star with an 8th-mag. companion, difficult in the smallest telescopes because of the brightness contrast.

continued

ANDROMEDA

TRIANGULUM

M76

869

884

φ

η

τ

ϑ

M34

π

16

γ

ι

κ

β Algol

ω

ϱ

17

ARIES

CAMELOPARDALIS

Algenib

α

σ

ν

1342

1444

δ ψ

ξ

o

1528

λ

ε

ζ

b1

b2

μ

48

58

AURIGA

Capella

TAURUS

ζ (zeta) Persei is a 3rd-mag. blue supergiant with a 9th-mag. companion for small telescopes.

η (eta) Persei is an attractive pair for small telescopes, consisting of orange and blue stars of 4th and 9th mag. in a star-sprinkled field.

Star clusters
NGC 869 and NGC 884, also known as h and χ (chi) Persei, are the famous Double Cluster, a related pair of star clusters that is one of the richest sights in the sky for small instruments. To the naked eye the two clusters appear together like a bright patch in the Milky Way. Binoculars show that they both consist of a scattering of bright stars, each cluster covering more than 0.5° of sky, with NGC 869 being the brighter and richer of the pair. A few red stars can be seen in NGC 884 with small telescopes, but none in NGC 869. Both clusters lie in a nearby spiral arm of the galaxy just over 7000 l.y. away.

M 34 (NGC 1039) is a large and bright cluster, easily resolved into individual stars by small telescopes.

Meteors
The Perseid meteors are the most glorious meteor shower of the year, producing a maximum of as many as 60 meteors per hour on August 12 or 13 each year. The Perseid meteors are bright, many of them exploding and leaving trains.

β Persei ~ Algol

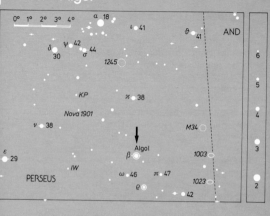

AND

PERSEUS

α 18
ι 41
ϑ 41
δ 30
ψ 42
σ 44
1245
KP
ϰ 38
Nova 1901
ν 38
M34
ε 29
Algol
β
1003
IW
ω 46
π 47
1023
ϱ
42

6
5
4
3
2

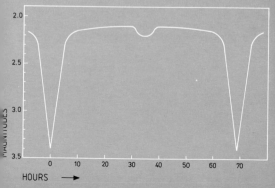

MAGNITUDES

2.0

2.5

3.0

3.5

0   10   20   30   40   50   60   70

HOURS ⟶

PHOENIX The Phoenix

A constellation of the southern celestial hemisphere, Phoenix represents the mythological bird that was reborn from its own ashes.

Variable star

ζ (zeta) Phoenicis is a complex variable and double star (see below), the brightest component of which is an eclipsing binary. It varies from mag. 3.9 to mag. 4.4 every 40 hours.

Double and multiple stars

β (beta) Phoenicis consists of a tight pair of 4th-mag. yellow stars needing apertures of 100mm and high magnification to be seen separately.

ζ (zeta) Phoenicis is a double-variable star. Small telescopes show it as a 4th-mag. blue-white star with an 8th-mag. companion; the brighter of the two stars is an eclipsing binary (see above).

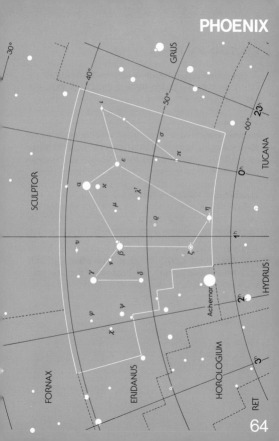

PICTOR The Painter's Easel

A faint and insignificant constellation of southern skies, Pictor's original title was Equuleus Pictoris, which has since been shortened to simply Pictor. Pictor contains little to interest the casual observer.

Nearby star

Kapteyn's Star is a 9th-mag. red dwarf, lying 12.7 l.y. away. It is noted for having the second-largest proper motion of any star. (The record for the largest proper motion of all goes to Barnard's Star in Ophiuchus.) Kapteyn's Star takes 414 years to move across 1° of sky.

Pictor shown under the name of Pluteum Pictoris on the 1801 star atlas of Johann Bode. *Royal Greenwhich Observatory*

PICTOR

CANIS MAJOR

COLUMBA

ERIDANUS

CAELUM

—————— 40°

PUPPIS

HOR

η² η¹

ζ

λ —— 50°

β

Canopus

ι

δ

γ

CARINA

—————— 60°

DORADO

α

RETICULUM

VOLANS

—————— 70°

7ʰ 6ʰ 5ʰ 4ʰ 3ʰ

HYDRUS

MENSA

65

PISCES The Fishes

Pisces is a constellation of the zodiac through which the Sun passes from mid-March to late April. The Sun crosses the celestial equator from south to north while in Pisces; this point is known as the vernal equinox, and is reached around March 21 each year. Pisces represents a pair of fishes tied together by their tails. It is a surprisingly faint constellation, its brightest stars being of only 4th mag.

Variable star
TX Piscium (19 Piscium) is a red giant irregular variable that fluctuates between 5th and 6th mag. It is notable for its deep red color.

Double stars
β (alpha) Piscium (Al Rischa, the cord) is a close pair of 4th and 5th-mag. white stars requiring 100mm aperture to separate them The stars are currently closing together, and hence becoming progressively more difficult to split.

ζ (zeta) Piscium is an easy pair of 5th and 6th-mag. stars for small telescopes.

ρ (rho) Piscium and 94 Piscium form an easy 5th-mag. binocular pair of white and orange stars.

ψ^1 (psi^1) Piscium is a wide pair of 5th-mag, blue-white stars for small telescopes.

continued

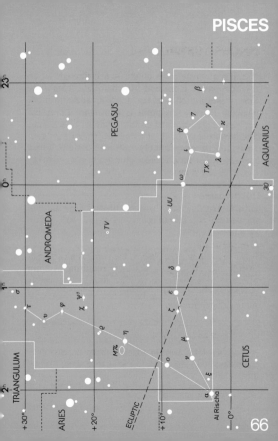

23ʰ

PEGASUS

β

γ

7

ϑ

κ

ι

λ

TX°

ω

0ʰ

30

UU

AQUARIUS

ANDROMEDA

°TV

δ

1ʰ

σ

ζ

τ

υ

φ

χ

ψ¹

ε

ζ

ϱ

η

μ

M74

ν

TRIANGULUM

2ʰ

ο

ξ

α

Al Rischa

CETUS

ARIES

+30°

+20°

+10°

0°

ECLIPTIC

66

PISCES AUSTRINUS The Southern Fish

A constellation of the southern sky, Pisces Austrinus is unremarkable but for its brightest star, Fomalhaut. This constellation was once also called Piscis Australis.

Bright star

α (alpha) Piscis Austrini (Fomalhaut, from the Arabic meaning fish's mouth) is a blue-white star of mag. 1.2, lying 22 l.y. away.

Double stars

β (beta) Piscis Austrini is a 4th-mag. white star with an unrelated 8th-mag. companion for small telescopes.

γ (gamma) Piscis Austrini is a pair of 4th and 8th-mag. stars, difficult to separate in small telescopes because of the contrast in brightness.

Pisces continued

Galaxy

M 74 (NGC 628) is a 10th-mag. spiral galaxy presented face-on, appearing impressive on long-exposure photographs but too faint to be seen well in small amateur telescopes.

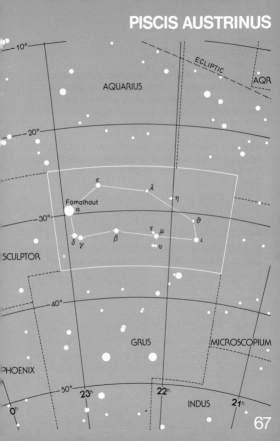

PUPPIS The Stern

A major constellation of the souther hemisphere of the sky, Puppis is the largest of the four sections into which the old constellation of Argo Navis, the ship of the Argonauts, was divided. It contains rich Milky Way star fields.

Variable stars

L² Puppis is a red giant semi-regular variable that fluctuates between 3rd and 6th mag. about every 140 days.

V Puppis is an eclipsing binary that varies from mag. 4.5 to mag. 5.1. every 35 hours.

Double stars

ζ (xi) Puppis is a 3rd-mag. yellow supergiant with a 5th-mag. orange binocular companion.

k Puppis is a neat pair of nearly equal 4th-mag. blue-white stars for small telescopes.

Star clusters

M 47 (NGC 2422) is a prominent binocular cluster of about 50 stars of 6th mag. and fainter.

NGC 2451 is a large and scattered group of bright stars centered on the 4th-mag. orange supergiant c Puppis.

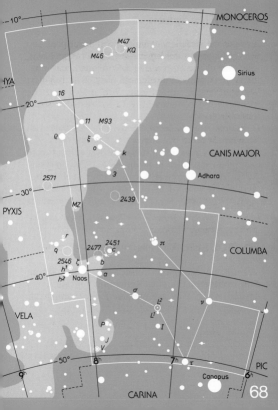

PUPPIS

MONOCEROS

−10°

M47
M46   KQ

Sirius

16

−20°

ıYA

11   M93

ϱ   ξ
         o   k

CANIS MAJOR

2571

3   Adhara

−30°

PYXIS   MZ   2439

r

q   2477   2451
              c
2546   ζ   b   π   COLUMBA
h¹
h²   Naos   a

VELA   σ   L²

                              L¹

P   I   v

J
V

−40°

−50°

8ʰ   7ʰ   τ   PIC
                              6ʰ

9ʰ   Canopus

CARINA   68

PYXIS The Compass

Pydix is the smallest and faintest of the four parts into which the large southern constellation of Argo Navis, the ship of the Argonauts, was divided; the other parts are Carina, Puppis, and Vela. The brightest stars of Pyxis are of only 4th mag., and the constellation contains little to interest the casual observer.

Recurrent nova

T Pyxidis is a recurrent nova that has erupted more often than any other: in 1890, 1902, 1920, 1944, and 1966. At its brightest it can reach 6th mag. but normally it slumbers at 14th mag. Further outbursts may be expected.

RETICULUM The Net

A small and insignificant constellation of the southern hemisphere of the sky, Reticulum represents an instrument used by astronomers for measuring star positions.

Double star

ζ (zeta) Reticuli is a naked-eye or binocular pair of identical 5th-mag. yellow stars similar to our own Sun. They lie 40 l.y. away.

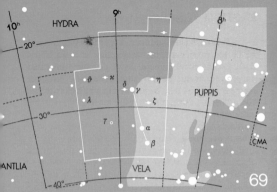

69

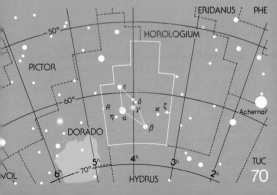

70

SAGITTA The Arrow

A constellation with a distinctive arrow shape, lying in the northern celestial hemisphere, Sagitta is the third-smallest constellation in the sky. One legend says that it represents an arrow shot from the bow of neighboring Hercules. Sagitta lies in a rich part of the Milky Way.

Double star
ζ (zeta) Sagittae is a pair of 5th and 9th-mag. stars for small telescopes.

Recurrent nova
WZ Sagittae is a nova that has been seen to flare up from 15th to 7th mag. in 1913 and 1946. Further outburst may well occur at any time.

Globular cluster
M 71 (NGC 6838) is a 7th-mag. globular cluster for binoculars and small telescopes in which it appears as a rounded misty patch. Some authorities regard it as a rich open cluster and not as a globular cluster.

CYGNUS

Vega

LYRA

+40°

+30°

VULPECULA

η

γ   ξ

WZ VZ   M71 δ   α

S   β

HERCULES

+20°

ELPHINUS

Altair

OPH

+10°

AQUILA

SERPENS
CAUDA

QR

20h

19h

0°

71

SAGITTARIUS The Archer

The Sun lies in this zodiacal constellation from late December to late January. Sagittarius represents a centaur aiming a bow and arrow at the heart of the neighboring scorpion, Scorpius. Sagittarius is different in character from the other celestial centaur, Centaurus, who is visualized as an altogether more peaceful creature. Sagittarius contains rich Milky Way star fields toward the center of our Galaxy, plus numerous clusters and nebulae.

Variable stars

W Sagittarii is a Cepheid variable that fluctuates between mags. 4.3 and 5.0 every 7 days 14 hours.

X Sagittarii is another Cepheid that varies from mag. 4.3 to 4.9 every 7 days.

Multiple star

β (beta) Sagittarii is a naked-eye double, consisting of two unrelated 4th-mag. stars. β¹ (beta¹) Sagittarii, the more northerly of the pair, has a 7th-mag. companion visible in small telescopes.

Star clusters

M 23 (NGC 6494) is a large binocular cluster covering nearly 0.5° of sky. Small telescopes resolve some of its 100 or so stars of mag. 9 and fainter.

continued

SAGITTARIUS

72

M 24 is not really a true star cluster; rather, it is the richest part of the Milky Way in Sagittarius, an elongated star cloud 2° long and 1° wide, visible to the naked eye. Binoculars and telescopes show it as a field of stardust.

M 25 (IC 4725) is a large, scattered binocular cluster of about 50 stars, of 6th mag. and fainter. Near the cluster's center is the yellow supergiant U Sagittarii, a Cepheid variable that ranges from mag. 6.3 to mag. 7.1 every 6 days 18 hours.

NGC 6530 is a binocular cluster of about 25 stars of mag. 7 and fainter lying in the Lagoon Nebula, M 8 (see below). The stars of the cluster have apparently formed recently from the surrounding gas.

Globular cluster

M 22 (NGC 6656) is a 6th-mag. binocular object with an apparent diameter half that of the full Moon. It is ranked as one of the finest globular clusters in the sky. Small telescopes reveal its noticeably elliptical outline, but apertures of at least 75mm are needed to resolve individual stars.

Nebulae

M 8 (NGC 6523), the Lagoon Nebula, is the best of the diffuse nebulae in Sagittarius and one of the finest in the entire sky It is visible to the naked eye as a 5th-mag. hazy patch of similar size to the Orion

Nebula. Binoculars and small telescopes show the cluster NGC 6530 (see page 194) that lies within it. The Nebula is divided by a dark rift, the so-called lagoon that gives the object its name, but apertures of 75mm and above are needed to show this well. On the other side of the rift from the cluster NGC 6530 are two prominent stars, the brighter of which is 6th-mag. 9 Sagittarii. Further to the side is the 5th-mag. orange giant 7 Sagittarii, but this is evidently a foreground object and is not associated with the nebula. The full complexity of the Lagoon Nebula and its pinkish-red color are brought out only on photographs.

M 17 (NGC 6618) is known variously as the Omega Nebula, the Horseshoe Nebula, and the Swan Nebula on account of its looped shape, although this is only defined in larger telescopes. In binoculars and small telescopes it appears as an elongated smudge, like the tail of a comet, with a sprinkling of faint stars along one side. This mini-cluster, which has no name of its own, is apparently associated with the nebula.

M 20 (NGC 6514), the Trifid Nebula, is a famous cloud of gas that takes its name from the lanes of dust that trisect it as seen on photographs. But small telescopes show only the multiple star at its heart, the two brightest components of which are 7th and 8th mag. Larger apertures are needed to see the nebulosity and dark dividing lanes. Note also the cluster M 21 (NGC 6531) in the same field of view.

SCORPIUS The Scorpion

A magnificent constellation of the zodiac, through which the Sun passes during the last week of November, Scorpius represents the scorpion whose sting killed Orion.

Bright star

α (alpha) Scorpii (Antares, from the Greek meaning rival of Mars, in reference to its strong red color) is a red supergiant 300 times the diameter of the Sun. It is also a semi-regular variable that fluctuates from about mag. 0.9 to mag. 1.1 over a period of several years. Antares has a 6th-mag. blue-green companion which requires at least 75mm aperture and steady air to be picked out from the glare of its primary.

Double and multiple stars

β (beta) Scorpii (Graffias, crab) is an impressive pair of 3rd and 5th-mag. stars for small telescopes.

$ζ^1$ $ζ^2$ (zeta^1 zeta^2) Scorpii is a naked-eye pair of unrelated stars. $ζ^1$ (zeta^1) is a 5th-mag. blue-white supergiant that may be an outlying member of the cluster NGC 6231 (see page 198), and $ζ^2$ (zeta^2) is a 4th-mag. orange giant nearer to us.

$μ^1$ $μ^2$ (mu^1 mu^2) Scorpii is a naked-eye pair, consisting of two blue-white stars of 3rd and 4th mag. $μ^1$ (mu^1) is an eclipsing binary with a range of only 0.3 mag.

continued

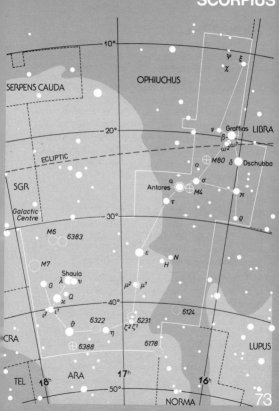

SCORPIUS

SERPENS CAUDA

OPHIUCHUS

ψ ξ
χ

ν Graffias LIBRA
β
ω² ω¹

ECLIPTIC

M80 δ Dschubba

SGR

α
ο
Antares σ M4
τ π

Galactic
Centre ϱ

M6 6383

ε N

M7 H

Shaula
G λ υ μ² μ¹

κ Q
ι² ι¹

CRA ϑ 6322 6124

η ζ²ζ¹ 6231

6388 6178 LUPUS

TEL 18ʰ ARA 17ʰ 16ʰ

10°

20°

30°

40°

50°

NORMA

73

ν (nu) Scorpii appears as a wide pair of 4th and 6th-mag. stars in small telescopes. Apertures of at least 75mm show that the fainter star is itself double.

ζ (xi) Scorpii is an excellent quadruple star for small telescopes, which show it as a 4th-mag. star with a 7th-mag. orange companion. Also visible in the same field is a wider duo of 7th and 8th-mag. stars, called Struve 1999, which are gravitationally connected to the first pair.

ω¹ ω² (omega¹ omega²) Scorpii is a naked-eye pair of unrelated 4th-mag. stars, one blue-white and the other a yellow giant.

Star clusters

M 6 (NGC 6405) is a binocular cluster covering 0.5o of sky, consisting of about 50 stars of mag. 7 and fainter seemingly arranged in radiating chains. The cluster's brightest star is a red giant variable, BM Scorpii, which reaches a maximum of mag. 6.

M 7 (NGC 6475) is a large and bright cluster visible to the naked eye covering 1° of sky. It is an excellent binocular object, consisting of 50 members of 6th mag. and fainter, arranged in a cruciform shape.

NGC 6231 is a naked-eye cluster of about 120 stars of 6th to 8th mag., like a mini-Pleiades, on a background of many fainter stars. The 5th-mag. star ζ¹ (zeta¹) Scorpii is thought to be an outlying member of the cluster. This is a glorious area for sweeping with binoculars; note a line of stars that leads from NGC 6231 to the very large and scattered binocular cluster H 12. The two clusters are definitely associated, both lying about 5000 l.y. away; the stars joining them outline a spiral arm of our Galaxy.

Globular cluster

M 4 (NGC 6121) is a large 7th-mag. globular cluster, among the closest to us of its kind, lying about 7000 l.y. away. It is visible in binoculars.

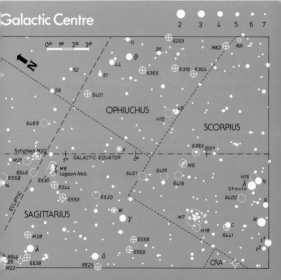

Galactic Centre

SCULPTOR The Sculptor

A faint constellation of the southern celestial hemisphere whose brightest stars are of only 4th mag., Sculptor contains the south galactic pole, i.e. the point 90° south of the plane of the Galaxy (the equivalent northern point lies in Coma Berenices).

Variable star
R Sculptoris is a red giant semi-regular variable noted for its deep red color. It varies between mags. 5.8 and 7.7 approximately every year.

Double stars
ε (epsilon) Sculptoris is a pair of 5th and 9th-mag. stars for small telescopes.

κ¹ (kappa¹) Sculptoris is a tight pair of 6th-mag. stars requiring apertures of at least 100mm and very high magnification.

Galaxies
NGC 55 is an 8th-mag. spiral galaxy presented nearly edge-on to us. It can be picked up in small telescopes as an elongated smudge of uneven brightness.

NGC 253, the brightest of the galaxies in Sculptor, is a 7th-mag. spiral visible in binoculars. It is tilted at an angle to us, so that it appears cigar-shaped in small instruments.

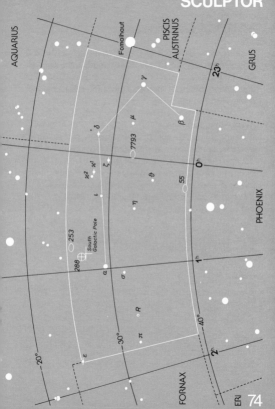

SCULPTOR

AQUARIUS

PISCIS AUSTRINUS

GRUS

Fomalhaut

23ʰ

γ

μ

δ

β

7793

ζ

χ²

χ¹

0ʰ

ι

ϑ

η

55

253

South Galactic Pole

288

PHOENIX

α

σ

1ʰ

R

40°

π

ε

2ʰ

20°

30°

FORNAX

ERI

74

SCUTUM The Shield

Scutum lies just south of the celestial equator, and is impressive despite its small size (the fifth-smallest constellation in the skies). It contains rich Milky Way star fields and is an attractive area for sweeping with binoculars.

Variable stars

δ (delta) Scuti is the prototype of a rare class of variable stars that undergo small pulsations in size every few hours, leading to minor changes in the brightness of the stars. δ (delta) Scuti itself varies every 4 hours 40 minutes from mag. 4.6 to 4.7, an amount that is barely detectable to the naked eye.

R Scuti is a somewhat unusual yellow giant variable star, usually classified as of the RV Tauri variety. It fluctuates semi-regularly between 5th and 8th mag.

Star cluster

M 11 (NGC 6705), the Wild Duck Cluster, is a beautiful group of about 200 stars of mag. 11 and fainter in a dense area of the Milky Way. It gets its popular name because its stars are arranged in a fan-shape, like a flight of wild ducks, with a brighter orange star at the apex. It is visible in all apertures, including binoculars, but larger instruments will resolve the individual stars more clearly.

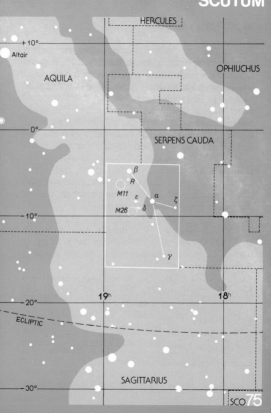

SCUTUM

HERCULES

OPHIUCHUS

Altair

AQUILA

+10°

SERPENS CAUDA

0°

β

R

M11

ε

α

ζ

M26

δ

−10°

γ

19h

18h

−20°

ECLIPTIC

SAGITTARIUS

−30°

SCO 75

SERPENS The Serpent

This is a unique constellation, for it is split into two separate halves (see map on pp.206–207). Serpens represents a snake coiled around the serpent holder, Ophiuchus. One side of Ophiuchus lies Serpens Caput, the serpent's head, which is the larger and more prominent half; on the other side of Ophiuchus lies Serpens Cauda, the serpent's tail. Despite being split in this way, the two halves of Serpens are counted as forming one constellation.

Double stars

β (beta) Serpentis consists of a pair of 4th and 9th-mag. stars divisible in small telescopes. Binoculars show an unrelated 7th-mag. star nearby.

δ (delta) Serpentis is a close pair of 4th and 5th-mag. stars for small telescopes with high magnification.

θ (theta) Serpentis is an easy pair of 4th and 5th-mag. white stars for small telescopes.

ν (nu) Serpentis is a 4th-mag. star with a wide 9th-mag. companion for small telescopes and binoculars.

Star clusters

τ¹ (tau¹) Serpentis is the brightest of a scattered group of 6th-mag. stars, best seen in binoculars, that extends toward κ (kappa) Serpentis.

M 16 (NGC 6611) is a cluster of over 50 stars of mag. 8 and fainter, visible in binoculars and small telescopes. It lies in the rich Milky Way region near the border with Scutum and Sagittarius. Under good conditions observers may detect a hint of nebulosity around the cluster. This is brought out well ohn long-exposure photographs (see below) which show M 16 tobe buried in a glorious cloud of glowing gas known as the Eagle Nebula. A feature of this nebula is the ribbon of darker dust that intrudes into it.

Globular cluster

M 5 (NGC 5904) is a 6th-mag. globular cluster rated as second-finest in the northern skies to M 13 in Hercules. M 5 is within range of binoculars as well as small telescopes, which show it as a hazy star, like the head of a comet. Larger telescopes reveal chains of stars radiating outward from its bright and dense center. In the same field of view if the 5th-mag. star 5 Serpentis, which has a 10th-mag. companion.

The Eagle Nebula is a faint cloud of gas surrounding the star cluster M 16 in Serpens. *Hale Observatories.*

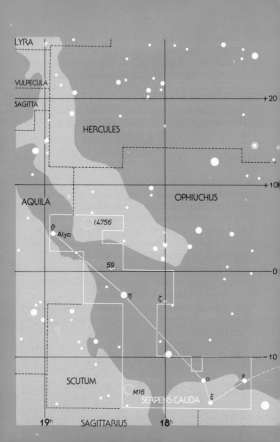

LYRA

VULPECULA

SAGITTA

+20

HERCULES

AQUILA   OPHIUCHUS

+10

I4756

ϑ
Alya

59   0

η   ζ

−10

SCUTUM   *M16*   o   ν

ξ

SERPENS CAUDA

19ʰ   SAGITTARIUS   18ʰ

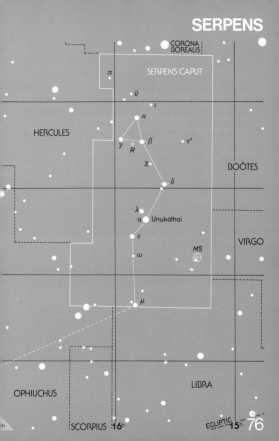

SEXTANS The Sextant

A barren constellation in the equatorial region of the sky, Sextans is almost indistinguishable on account of its faintness. It represents the sextant, an instrument used by astronomers for measuring the positions of stars before the days of the telescope. The brightest star in Sextans is of only mag. 4.5.

Double star

17-18 Sextantis are a binocular pair of 6th-mag. stars, one an orange giant and the other blue-white.

Galaxy

NGC 3115 is a small 10th-mag. galaxy seen edge-on so that it appears spindle-shaped. Moderate-sized telescopes are needed to show it well.

Sextans, shown under its original title, Sextans Uraniae, on the 1801 atlas of Johann Bode. *Royal Greenwich Observatory.*

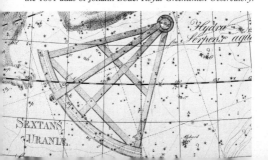

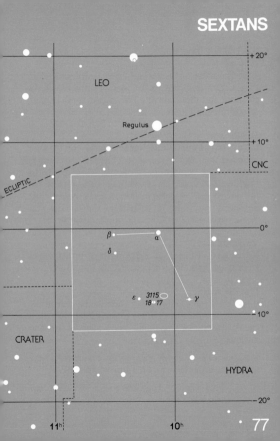

SEXTANS

LEO

+ 20°

Regulus

+ 10°

CNC

ECLIPTIC

0°

β   α

δ

ε   3115
   18 · 17   γ

- 10°

CRATER

HYDRA

- 20°

11ʰ   10ʰ

TAURUS The Bull

A constellation of the zodiac, through which the Sun passes from mid-May to late June, Taurus represents the head and shoulders of a bull, depicted as charging at neighboring Orion.

Bright star

α (alpha) Tauri (Aldebaran, from the Arabic meaning the follower, i.e. of the Pleiades star cluster) is an orange-colored giant of mag. 0.9, the 13th-brightest star in the sky. It represents the glinting red eye of the bull. Aldebaran lies 68 l.y. away, so that although it appears to be part of the Hyades star cluster (see p.212) it is actually much closer to us.

Variable star

λ (lambda) Tauri is an eclipsing binary that varies from mag. 3.4 to mag. 4.1 every 4 days.

Double stars

$θ^1$ $θ^2$ (theta^1 theta^2) Tauri is a wide double star in the Hyades (see p.212), divisible by binoculars or naked eye, consisting of white and yellow stars of 3rd and 4th mag.

κ (kappa) Tauri, of 4th mag., forms a wide naked-eye or binocular double with 67 Tauri, of 5th mag.

$σ^1$ $σ^2$ (sigma^1 sigma^2) Tauri are a wide binocular duo of 5th-mag. white stars.

continued

ARIES

ECLIPTIC

+20°

CETUS

+10°

0°

5

ξ

o

10

η

BU

M45
Pleiades

4ʰ

ψ

φ

χ

37

ω

ν

κ

Hyades

δ

γ

χ

ψ

μ

ERIDANUS

τ

ε

68

α
Aldebaran

θ¹

θ²

π

90

88

1647

σ²

σ¹

5ʰ

AURIGA

1746

ι

CE

β
El Nath

M1

ζ

GEMINI

Betelgeuse

ORION

78

φ (phi) Tauri is a 5th-mag. orange giant with an unrelated 9th-mag. companion visible in small telescopes.

χ (chi) Tauri is an attractive pair of 5th and 8th-mag. blue and gold stars for small telescopes.

Star clusters

The Hyades is a very large and scattered cluster of stars, arranged in a V-shape, that makes up the face of the bull. The cluster contains about 200 stars, the brightest dozen or so of which are visible to the naked eye. Because of its considerable size, covering 5° of sky, the Hyades is best studied with binoculars. The cluster lies about 150 l.y. away. Note that the bright star Aldebaran is not a member of the cluster but is actually a foreground object of only about half the distance.

M 45, the Pleiades, is the finest star cluster in the sky. To the naked eye it appears as a slightly hazy group of about six stars, but binoculars and small telescopes bring many more stars into view, covering more than 1° of sky. Probably over 200 stars belong to the cluster which lies 415 l.y. away, further than the Hyades. The brightest member of the Pleiades cluster is 3rd-mag. η (eta) Tauri (Alcyone). Under very clear conditions some faint nebulosity may be seen in
continued

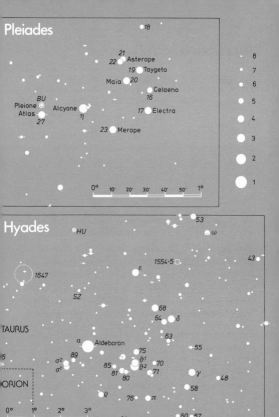

TELESCOPIUM The Telescope

An unremarkable constellation of the southern sky, Telescopium is a poor tribute to the astronomer's most fundamental instrument, the telescope.

Double star

δ^1 δ^2 (delta^1 delta^2) Telescopii are a binocular pair of unrelated 5th-mag. blue-white stars.

Taurus continued

binoculars and small telescopes around 23 Tauri (Merope). Long-exposure photographs show that the whole cluster is enveloped in faint nebulosity, the remains of the cloud from which the stars formed.

Nebula

M 1 (NGC 1952) is the Crab Nebula, the remains of a star that was seen to explode as a supernova in A.D. 1054, and one of the most famous objects in the heavens. It is a challenging object for small telescopes, appearing as an elliptical 8th-mag. hazy patch. Its popular name was given from its supposed resemblance to the claws of a crab. Although not as spectacular in small instruments as it appears on photographs, it is worth seeking out as the brightest example of a supernova remnant.

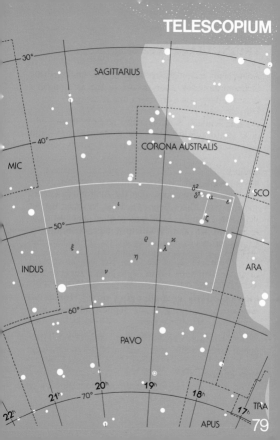

SAGITTARIUS

30°

CORONA AUSTRALIS

40°

MIC

SCO

δ²
δ¹ α
ε
ι
ζ

50°

ϱ
ξ
λ κ
η
ν

INDUS

ARA

60°

PAVO

22ʰ   21ʰ   20ʰ   19ʰ   18ʰ   17ʰ

70°

APUS

TRA

TRIANGULUM The Triangle

Triangulum is a small constellation of distinctive shape in the northern sky.

Double star

ι (iota) Trianguli is an attractive pair of 5th and 7th-mag. golden and blue stars, divisible at high magnification in small telescopes.

Galaxy

M 33 (NGC 598) is the third-largest member of our Local Group of galaxies, after the Andromeda Galaxy and our own Milky Way. It is large (covering 0.5° of sky), but faint. M 33 is best seen in binoculars, or wide-field telescopes with low magnification, on account of its low contrast against the sky background. A clear, dark night is vital to find M 33.

TRIANGULUM AUSTRALE
The Southern Triangle

A small but easily identified southern constellation, Triangulum Australe's three main stars are of 2nd and 3rd mag.

Star cluster

NGC 6025 is a binocular group of about 30 stars of mag. 7 and fainter, 2000 l.y. away.

TRIANGULUM

Algol

PERSEUS

3ʰ

2ʰ ANDROMEDA

1ʰ

+40°

R°

δ β
γ ε

ι

M33

α

+30°

ARIES

PISCES

80

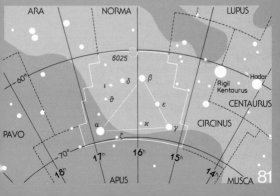

TRIANGULUM AUSTRALE

ARA NORMA LUPUS

6025

60°

ι δ β

ϑ

Rigil
Kentaurus

Hadar

α ε CENTAURUS

κ γ CIRCINUS

PAVO

70° ζ

18ʰ 17ʰ 16ʰ 15ʰ 14ʰ MUSCA

APUS 81

TUCANA The Toucan

Tucana is a constellation of the southern sky, containing few bright stars but marked by the presence of the Small Magellanic Cloud and the globular cluster known as 47 Tucanae.

Double and multiple stars

β (beta) Tucanae is a multiple star. Binoculars show it as a wide double of 4th and 5th mags., while in small telescopes the brighter component is itself seen as an easy pair of 5th-mag. blue-white stars.

δ (delta) Tucanae is a 4th-mag. star with a 9th-mag. companion for small telescopes.

κ (kappa) Tuacanae is a double star for small telescopes consisting of components of 5th and 7th mag.

Globular clusters

47 Tucanae (NGC 104) is regarded as the second finest globular cluster in the sky, beaten only by ω (omega) Centauri. It is visible to the naked eye as a hazy 5th-mag. star. Binoculars clearly show the increase in brightness toward its star-packed core, while telescopes of 100mm aperture begin to resolve the brightest of its 100,000 or more individual stars. The cluster covers nearly 0.5° of sky and is a showpiece object for all sizes of instrument. It is a relatively close globular, about 20,000 l.y. away.

continued

NGC 362 is a 6th-mag. globular cluster visible in binoculars at the edge of the Small Magellanic Cloud. It is not in fact part of it, but is a foreground object lying about 40,000 l.y. away in our own Galaxy.

Galaxy

The Small Magellanic Cloud (NGC 292) is the smaller of the two companion galaxies of our Milky Way. It is also the more distant, located 230,000 l.y. away. It is visible to the naked eye as a misty patch over 3° long, shaped somewhat like a tadpole. Binoculars and small telescopes resolve individual stars, clusters and glowing nebulae in the Small Magellanic Cloud.

Tucana, the Toucan, as depicted by Johann Bode on his star atlas of 1801. *Royal Greenwich Observatory.*

The Small Magellanic cloud is an elongated splash of stars visible to the naked eye in Tucana. At the bottom is the bright globular cluster 47 Tucanae. *Royal Observatory Edinburgh.*

URSA MAJOR The Great Bear

The third-largest constellation, lying in the northern hemisphere of the sky, Ursa Major contains a group of seven stars that make up the familiar figure of the Plough or Big Dipper. The stars β (beta) and α (alpha) Ursae Majoris point to the north pole star, Polaris.

Double and multiple stars

ζ (zeta) Ursaw Majoris (Mizar, from the Arabic meaning girdle), of 2nd mag. is one of the most famous multiple stars in the sky. Keen eyesight or simple binoculars show a 4th-mag. companion, Alcor (80 Ursaw Majoris). In small telescopes another 4th-mag star is visible closer to Mizar. Each of these stars is also a spectroscopic binary.

ζ (xi) Ursae Majoris is a pair of 4th and 5th-mag. yellow stars that orbit each other every 60 years. At their widest apart in 1975 they were divisible in small telescopes, but at their closest, around 1992, they required at least 150mm aperture to split.

Galaxies

M 81 (NGC 3031) is an 8th-mag. spiral galaxy that appears in small telescopes as an elliptical patch with a noticeably brighter core. Photographs show it to be one of the most beautiful spirals in the sky. Under good conditions both M 81 and its partner M 82 are visible in binoculars.

continued

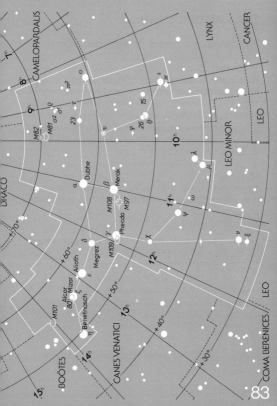

URSA MAJOR

83

URSA MINOR The Little Bear

This contellation contains the north celestial pole.

Pole star
α (alpha) Ursae Minoris (Polaris) is a yellow supergiant that lies within 1° of the north celestial pole. Precession will take it closest to the true pole in about A.D. 2100. Polaris is a Cepheid variable, fluctuating between mags. 2.1 and 2.2 every 4 days. It is also a double star, with a 9th-mag. companion visible in small telescopes.

Double star
γ (gamma) Ursae Minoris is a 3rd-mag. blue-white star with an unrelated 5th-mag. star, 11 Ursae Minoris, nearby, visible to the naked eye or in binoculars.

Ursa Major continued

M 82 (NGC 3034) is a 9th-mag. galaxy near M 81 (see previous page) presented edge-on to us so that it appears as an elongated smudge in small telescopes.

M 101 (NGC 5457) is a 9th-mag. spiral galaxy, face-on to us. Photographs show it to be an impressive galaxy with far-flung spiral arms, but only the brightest central part is visible in small telescopes.

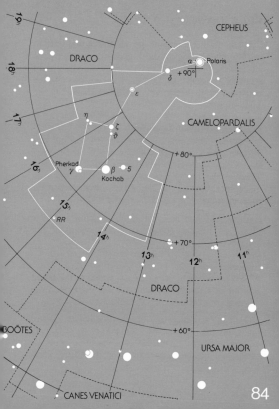

URSA MINOR

CEPHEUS

DRACO

CAMELOPARDALIS

Polaris
α
δ
+90°
ε
η
ζ
ϑ
Pherkad
γ
β
5
Kochab
RR
+80°

BOÖTES

DRACO

URSA MAJOR

CANES VENATICI

+70°

+60°

19ʰ

18ʰ

17ʰ

16ʰ

15ʰ

14ʰ

13ʰ

12ʰ

11ʰ

84

VELA The Sails

Vela was formerly part of the ancient constellation of Argo Navis, the ship of the Argonauts; the other parts are Carina, Puppis, and Pyxis. Since it is only part of a former constellation, Vela contains no stars labelled α (alpha) or β (beta). Vela lies in a rich part of the Milky Way.

Double and multiple stars

γ (gamma) Velorum is a binocular duo of 2nd and 4th-mag. stars, the brightest of which is the brightest star of the Wolf-Rayet type (see p.1544). γ (gamma) Velorum also has wider companions of 9th and 10th mags., making this an interesting multiple star for small apertures.

δ (delta) Velorum is a tight double star for apertures of at least 100mm, consisting of components of 2nd and 6th mag.

Star clusters

IC 2391 is a bright knot of stars, visible to the naked eye but best seen in binoculars, scattered around the 4th-mag. star o (omicron) Velorum.

NGC 2547 is a binocular cluster of about 50 stars of mag. 7 and fainter.

VELA

PUPPIS
CARINA
PYXIS
ANTLIA
CENTAURUS
HYDRA
CRUX
VOL
PIC
8h
9h
10h
11h
40°
50°
60°
AH
2547
1.2395
1.2391
1.2488
3132
3201
3228

VIRGO The Virgin

Virgo is a constellation of the zodiac, in which the Sun lies from late September to the end of October. The Sun is in Virgo at the time of the autumnal equinox, i.e. the time when the Sun moves into the southern celestial hemisphere; this happens around September 23 each year. Virgo is the second-largest constellation in the sky. In various legends she represents the goddess of justice or the goddess of the harvest.

Bright star

α (alpha) Virginis (Spica, ear of wheat) is a blue-white star of mag. 1.0, 260 l.y. away.

Double stars

γ (gamma) Virginis consists of a pair of 4th-mag. yellow-white stars that orbit each other every 172 years. As seen from Earth they are currently closing together. By the year A.D. 2000 they will need apertures of 100mm to split them, and at their closest together around A.D. 2007 they will be indivisible in amateur telescopes; thereafter they will widen out again.

θ (theta) Virginis is a pair of 4th and 9th mag. stars for small telescopes.

τ (tau) Virginis is a 4th-mag. star with a wide unrelated 9th- mag. companion for small telescopes.

continued

LEO

CRATER

ω

ν

ξ

β

12ʰ

ο

π

COMA BERENICES

M90 M85

M84

M49

M61

η

M89

M87

M104

CHI

Porrima

CORVUS

M60

M59 M58

θ

δ

γ

ECLIPTIC

ψ

13ʰ

Vindemiatrix

ε

σ

ϑ

Spica

α

CW

ζ

14ʰ

τ

ι

κ

ET

HYDRA

BOOTES

ν

φ

λ

μ

LIBRA

109

15ʰ

110

+10°

0°

−10°

−20°

Galaxies

Virgo contains a major cluster of galaxies lying about 65 million l.y. away. The Virgo Cluster of galaxies spills over the border into neighboring Coma Berenices, so sometimes it is known as the Virgo-Coma Cluster. The chart opposite shows the brightest members of the cluster, and the most interesting members are described below. These can be located as faintly glowing patches of light in small telescopes.

M 49 (NGC 4472) is a 9th-mag. elliptical galaxy.

M 58 (NGC 4579) is a 9th-mag. spiral galaxy.

M 60 (NGC 4649) is a 9th-mag. elliptical galaxy.

M 84 (NGC 4374) and M 86 (NGC 4406) are a pair of 9th-mag. elliptical galaxies visible in the same field.

M 87 (NGC 4486) is a giant elliptical galaxy, also known as the radio source Virgo A. A giant black hole is thought to lie at the heart of this powerful galaxy.

M 104 (NGC 4594), the Sombrero Galaxy, is not a member of the Virgo Cluster and lies at about half the cluster's distance. It is a spiral that appears somewhat like a sombrero hat on photographs.

Virgo/Coma Galaxy-cluster

3 4 5 6 7

LEO

23

M64
35
26
20
2
5

24   M85
4394   4293
11
4450
4350   M100
36
32 27
4651
3
4710   95
M91 M88
M99
4866   4459   M98   COMA BERENICES
29   4689   4477
26   M90 4473
4654   M89   4438   M86
41   M84 4215   VIRGO
34   M58 M87 4388
ε   4762 4754 M60   4429
Vindemiatrix   4568 4371
ϱ 27   20   4178
33   4596   4442   12
4578
4598   4483
32   4535   O
4526   M49
4570 4365
31 R
EP
4261   11
17
M61
35 4665   4496 4457   16
4900   37   4636   4123
4643
10
0° 1° 2° 3° 4° 5°   4179
SS

VOLANS The Flying Fish

A small and faint constellation in the south polar region of the sky, Volans was originally known as Piscis Volans. Its brightest stars are only of 4th mag.

Double stars

γ (gamma) Volantis is an attractive pair of white and golden-yellow stars of 4th and 6th mag. for small telescopes.

ε (epsilon) Volantis is a 4th-mag. blue-white star with a close 8th-mag. companion visible in small telescopes.

Volans, shown under its original title of Piscis Volans, on Johann Bode's 1801 star atlas. *Royal Greenwich Observatory*

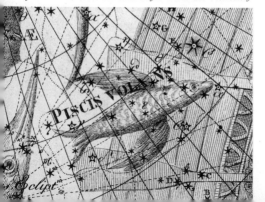

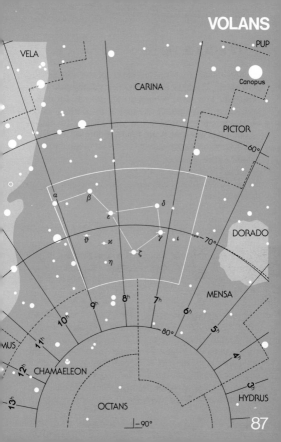

VOLANS

PUP

VELA

CARINA

Canopus

PICTOR

60°

α

β

δ

ε

ϑ κ

ζ

γ ι

70°

DORADO

η

MENSA

9ʰ

8ʰ

7ʰ

6ʰ

5ʰ

10ʰ

80°

11ʰ

4ʰ

MUS

12ʰ

CHAMAELEON

3ʰ

13ʰ

OCTANS

HYDRUS

−90°

87

VULPECULA The Fox

A faint but far from uninteresting constellation in the northern hemisphere of the sky, Vulpecula was originally known as Vulpecula cum Anser, the fox and goose. In Vulpecula the first of the flashing radio stars known as pulsars was discovered by radio astronomers at Cambridge, England, in 1967.

Double star

α (alpha) Vulpeculae is a 4th-mag. red giant with an unrelated 6th-mag. companion, 8 Vulpeculae, visible in binoculars.

Star cluster

The Coathanger is a binocular group of stars with an amusing shape, situated along the border with Sagitta. Its most remarkable feature is a straight line of six stars of 6th and 7th mag. Four stars extending from the center of this line form a hook that completes the coathanger shape.

Planetary nebula

M 27 (NGC 6853), the Dumbbell Nebula, is a large and bright planetary nebula, reputedly the most conspicuous of its kind. It is visible in binoculars and telescopes, appearing as an extended misty green glow covering about one quarter the diameter of the full Moon. It takes its name from its double-lobed shape as seen through large telescopes and on photographs.

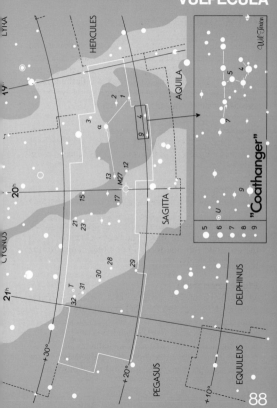

VULPECULA

"Coathanger"

Will Tirion

88

Index

Page numbers in bold denote photographs or diagrams

238